In this book you will find:

- How to maximize your chances for successfully moving your idea to market on a limited budget!

- Where to find free or nearly free help!

- Tips on how to pace your expenditures!

- When you must spend money and when you don't have to!

- How to know whom you can trust and whom you should *not* trust!

- Where to find the money to help you pursue your invention!

- Tips for toy inventors!

- *COUPONS WORTH OVER $500.00 ON ESSENTIAL INVENTOR SERVICES!*

D1450364

Inventing
On a Shoestring
Budget™!

Insider tips for bringing your product to market without breaking the bank!

Barbara Russell Pitts & Mary Russell Sarao

Successful Inventors, Speakers and Inventor Mentors

Second Sight Publishing

608
Pit

ISBN: 0-9785222-0-6

First Edition
Cataloging in publication data:

Pitts, Barbara Russell, 1941 –
Sarao, Mary Russell, 1946 –

Inventing on a Shoestring Budget™: Insider tips for bringing your product
to market without breaking the bank! /Barbara Russell Pitts and Mary Russell
Sarao.

p.cm.
Includes index
Library of Congress Control Number: 2006903288
ISBN: 0-9785222-0-6

1. Inventing—Handbooks, manuals, etc. 2. Inventing - Finance. I. Title:
Inventing on a Shoestring Budget™: Insider tips for bringing your product to
market without breaking the bank!

Cover design by Fred Fleming

This publication is designed to provide accurate and authoritative information
with regard to the subject matter covered. It is sold with the understanding that
the publisher is not engaged in rendering legal, accounting, or other professional
advice. If legal advice or other expert assistance is required, the services of a
competent professional person should be sought.
---From a *Declaration of Principles* jointly adopted by a Committee of the
American Bar Association and a Committee of Publishers and Associations

Second Sight Publishing
Dallas, Texas
www.asktheinventors.com

Whether you are

a Shoestring Budget™ Inventor

by necessity or by choice . . .

It's the smart thing to do.

This book is dedicated to You!

Acknowledgements

This book is truly a labor of love, because we did it out of our desire to share money-saving secrets with our fellow inventors across the country. It is also a labor of love because of the outpouring of assistance we received from experts in every area from patent professionals to publishing professionals. It has been a joy to write because we really found out who our friends are when we asked for assistance. We are blessed with knowledgeable friends! All of the experts that we approached gave enthusiastically of their time and knowledge to help make this book happen. So, even though our names are on the cover, this book was a team effort that could not have come together without the contributions of each one of them.

First on our list to thank is Barb Doyen, our literary agent. Even though we elected to write this book on our own without a publishing contract, Barb generously offered us advice and support in our efforts. Just being associated with Barb has given us tremendous credibility as writers and made us realize that we could do this and succeed.

Thanks, Fred Fleming, for taking our idea and translating it into a book cover that gets our message across perfectly. You are indeed an artist! As if that were not enough, you saved the day for us with your generous offer to format the manuscript into a real book. Fred, you have our undying gratitude! And thanks to Susan Fleming for her help with proofreading our manuscript.

Thanks also to Alan Thiele, Esq., who taught us some money-saving tips in the area of patents and who took the time to read and check our patent chapter for accuracy and precision. Alan, you are a tremendous asset and we appreciate you! Thanks to Guy V. Manning, Esq., another good friend and great attorney, for assistance with that chapter. Your patience in taking the time to give us detailed explanations of legal intricacies helps us to help others. And our special gratitude goes to our good friend and team member at Texas Inventors' Association, Robert Wise, Esq.. Bob, your unselfish sharing of your time and legal expertise have made our organization a dynamic place for inventors and you have been a tremendous continuing source of legal information for us personally.

And, there are those who have provided discounts for our coupon pages. Your generosity is making it easier for Shoestring Budget™ Inventors everywhere. Among those who are discounting their goods and services to help our inventors stretch their inventing dollars are Fred Fleming, Randall Landreneau, Ron Brown, Mike Marra, Rick Patino, Robert Mason, Esq., Randy Moyse, Jeff Crilley, Kevin Prince, Inventors' Digest Magazine, United Inventors Association, and the Wisconsin Innovation Service Center.

To all of these people and any others that we may have inadvertently omitted, we are deeply grateful!

Contents

Introduction

Inventing on a Shoestring Budget™! If that sounds too good to be true, rest assured it is not. There are many free or nearly free resources, cost cutting tips, and sources of help, financial and otherwise, inventors on a budget could and should avail themselves of during every step of the process.

This book was written by us, two shoestring budget inventors who were forced to find cost saving methods in order to keep our invention, Ghostline®, moving toward the market or give up on our idea. For us, giving up was not an option. We felt compelled to get our product on the market. If your product nags at you, like our product nagged us, but you do not have a lot of cash to spend developing, protecting and marketing it, then this is the book for you! This book is not intended to be a complete guide to independent inventing but a guide to direct you to sources of free or nearly free help as well as cost cutting methods every step of the way. There are many books that guide the inventor through the steps involved in the process, including our previous book, The Everything Inventions & Patents Book. This book was not written to replace those more detailed volumes. Independent inventors on a shoestring budget should avail themselves of both types of books.

Since we succeeded in getting Ghostline® to market we have become deeply involved in the independent inventor community. We have lectured extensively on the different aspects of inventing and marketing at invention seminars and to inventor groups around the country. We have been interviewed on television and radio programs as well as written about in newspapers across the country. In 2005, our first book, The Everything Inventions & Patents Book, was published. In our appearances before new inventors, the question we are most asked is, "How can I get my idea developed, protected and marketed on my limited budget?" Being blessed by having done that very thing, we feel uniquely qualified to guide you through those steps. During our journey, we have learned even more ways independent inventors can cut costs and save money while still moving their inventions forward. We want to share all we have learned with you.

In the interest of clarity and ease of reading this book, we have referred to all inventors by the male gender terms "he," "his," and so on. This is in no way intended to be offensive to female readers or to indicate that we believe all independent inventors are male. We are living proof that they are not. So, please accept these gender references as they are intended... for all inventors, regardless of whether they are male or female.

Our greatest desire is for this book to give you the resources and encouragement to move your product to market. At this writing, Ghostline® sells in excess of $10 million dollars per year. It was a simple idea developed by us, two middle-aged sisters who had no previous inventing experience and extremely limited financial resources. We now live the life of our dreams, writing and helping other inventors. We are living proof that Shoestring Budget™ inventing is not a fantasy. We did it and you can too!

 We've chosen the lightbulb -- the universal symbol of innovative ideas -- and inserted an exclamation mark as a means of calling attention to really important passages throughout this book.

CHAPTER ONE

Inventing on a Shoestring Budget™?
You Can Do It!

What is a Shoestring Budget™?

What exactly do we mean by a "shoestring budget?" Does this mean that if you have a wonderful idea but no money at all, you can somehow get your product developed, protected and marketed? Unfortunately, no, it doesn't. There may be a case somewhere of some millionaire who was so taken with someone's inspired idea that he immediately agreed to underwrite the whole thing, making the person with the original idea rich beyond his wildest dreams . . . but we haven't heard about it.

By shoestring budget, what we do mean is if you are like most of us, you do not have a lot of disposable income to spend on a highly speculative project. We know that to you your invention idea is probably a sure thing but in the world of inventing, there is no such thing as a sure thing. There are entirely too many variables to make any invention idea a guaranteed success. Keep in mind that the term "shoestring budget" includes the word budget. That means that you will have to spend some money on your invention. If you really believe in your idea, however, you should be willing to invest something in it, no matter how limited your resources might be.

Your shoestring budget may consist of a relatively small amount of money that you have been able to squirrel away for hobbies, entertainment or eating out. Your shoestring budget may consist of money from your savings. It might be small loans or investments from family and friends. We would strongly urge you not to spend money that you should allocate elsewhere such as for food, lodging, and everyday expenses. You may think these statements are foolish but there have been want-to-be inventors who have done exactly that. We have heard from inventors who got second mortgages, sold their cars and property to finance their inventions only to have the inventions fail, and as a result they jeopardized their families' financial security. Your invention may be the best thing since sliced bread but don't bet the farm on it. Many a great invention has failed to make it to the marketplace or in the marketplace due to variables that were completely out of the inventor's control.

How much money do you need to start?

Your shoestring budget does not have to be a significant amount of money that is available at the start of the project. It can be money that is saved and gathered as you move through the process, a bit here and a bit there. It should come as a great relief to you to realize that you do not have to have all the money you will eventually need right at the beginning of your project.

Even though you may not have a substantial surplus amount of money, the great news is that the American Dream is alive and well. If you have an idea for the next great innovation, there are many, many free and cost-cutting ways to get through the necessary steps of researching, developing, protecting and marketing your wonderful invention and we are here to share them with you.

By the time you have finished this book, there should be no "sticker shock" involved in your project. You will know what steps you can do for no money at all, and there are several of those, thanks to the Internet and a little creativity and initiative on your part. You will know where you can get free and very low cost legal advice. You will know where to get free help with your research, free business advice, and what you will need to know about creating your prototype and presenting it for licensing if that is your goal. If your plan is to build a business around your invention, you will know the sources of free or nearly free help to support you in that process. You will know where and how to look for financial assistance if you absolutely cannot go it alone.

Too many inventors think that because they have a great idea someone will just step up and invest in it. Think again. If someone does agree to invest money in your project you can be sure that they will want to know that you have invested your money, even if it is a modest amount, and your sweat equity in your invention before risking their money.

You will know how to protect yourself against the crooks who bilk millions of dollars each year from hapless inventors. You will understand the different types of protection and the least expensive ways to protect your invention. In short, you will join the ranks of the Shoestring Budget™Inventors.

We often hear novice inventors say that they have a great idea and that their plan is to sell the idea to some manufacturer for royalties. Their thinking seems to be that their total contribution to the arrangement is the wonderful idea and that the manufacturer will take the idea and do all of the research, development and protection and will pay them a handsome royalty. If this is your plan, you need to know that manufacturers do not buy ideas. Many of them do enter into licensing arrangements for developed and protected inventions. This means that you will need to invest some time and some amount of money in the research, development and protection of your idea if you want to get the serious

3

attention of a manufacturer.

How much money will I need?

So, just how much does it cost to develop and bring a new product to market? That shadowy financial area of patenting can be frightening for even the most determined of independent inventors. You want to have at least a ballpark idea of how much it is going to cost before you embark on such a project. Obviously, there are variables such as what your invention is and how much of the process you can do that make it impossible to give exact estimates. But, we will go out on a limb and tell you that with the secrets we will share in this book you will be able to make a pretty close determination of what your costs will be very early in your project.

You can estimate how much your invention will cost by looking at these factors:

- The complexity of developing the idea into a product.

- Whether you have the time and desire to do your own research and prototyping.

- Whether you are willing to educate yourself and do some of the work that a nonprofessional can reasonably do toward the protection of your invention.

Careful manipulation of the above factors can sometimes result in your new product being developed and presented for licensing for under $5,000.00, and in some cases well under that amount. As you read through the chapters of this book, you will not only learn the vital basic steps in the inventing process, but you will find financial shortcuts for almost every step in that process.

The most expensive part of the entire inventing process is likely to be the patent. There are ways to trim your budget here, too, without sacrificing your protection. But, even if you find that, due to the nature of your invention and your personal situation regarding your time constraints or knowledge, the financial outlay for your patent will be significant, the good news is that the patent process is a slow one. The payments are spaced out at intervals, giving you lots of time to accumulate the money for those payments.

We are Shoestring Budget™ inventors!

Our **Ghostline®** story is a classic example of Shoestring Budget™ inventing. In 1994, Mary had an actual dream of our product, a poster board that had faint lines printed on it, eliminating the need for measuring and drawing lines before beginning a poster project. Neither of us possessed any previous inventing experience but we knew that we would have to protect the invention and that we would first have to make sure that it was really ours to protect. To us, this meant making the rounds of the local stores that sold poster board to be sure that we didn't find the product. We didn't find it. Whew! First hurdle behind us!

We had read an article in a magazine about a successful inventor and it stated that all inventors should keep a journal beginning at the idea stage. So, we purchased an inexpensive blank, lined composition book with stitched-in pages to use for our inventors' journal and began keeping notes of the idea and our progress with the research, what we found in the stores and the things we were learning.

Next, since we did not have Internet access at the time, we went to our local branch of the United States Patent and Trademark Depository Library to do a preliminary patent search. We had never done a patent search before, or even been inside a patent library, but the patent librarians were well trained and extremely helpful. We spent several days poring over the patent books and printing out a few patents that looked similar to our idea. So far, our market search and our preliminary patent search had cost us only a few days of our time, some gasoline, and a couple of dollars for the journal and a few photocopies.

We learned from a librarian about the **United States Patent and Trademark Office's Disclosure Document program.** *This is a first step in documenting and dating your ownership of an idea and it costs only $10.00 to file. We took advantage of that opportunity. Go to:*

www.uspto.gov/web/offices/pac/disdo.html

for information on this program. You will find more information on Disclosure Documents in Chapter 5," Document Your Idea and Start Protecting It"

During the same period when we were doing our patent research at the library, we were also experimenting with our idea by making light lines on poster boards with different pencils, pens and inks. We enlisted the help of a friend, a retired printer, who advised us at no charge and told us of a place where we could educate ourselves about ink formulations. We spent some time learning about inks and their properties at an ink manufacturer's plant . . . again, at no charge.

At this point, we went to a printer and, under protection of a contractor non-disclosure form (see Chapter 6), we pooled $1,000.00 from our savings accounts and had an initial batch made of the poster boards with the grid printed on it. We found a patent attorney who allowed us the first visit without charge in order to determine if he would take us on as clients. Many patent attorneys do this, another freebie! It was at this point that, in our naiveté, we made a costly error. We allowed the attorney to obtain our professional patent search for us. We paid $700.00 for a search that would have cost us around $250.00 if we had gone directly to a search firm, rather than through an attorney. But, we didn't have this book to tell us that!

While it is possible to file for a patent without conducting a professional search, it is a foolhardy thing to do. The USPTO will gladly take your filing fees if you are willing to take the risk that your application will be rejected because it is too similar to an existing patent.

When our professional search came back indicating that we were free to pursue the idea without infringing an existing patent, we hired the patent attorney to write and file a utility patent application. At that time, the initial cost to have the application written and filed was $3,500.00. We again raided our savings accounts. But now we were patent pending and could begin marketing our product.

We began by making the rounds of small teacher stores and office supply stores, selling small batches of product, thereby replenishing our finances. Selecting a name for our invention, we took some of these funds and returned to the attorney to file for a federal trademark. Since our plan was to license our product to a large manufacturer, we proceeded in several directions at this point. We donated some product to area schools, leaving questionnaires, thereby obtaining a free marketing survey. And, we began contacting manufacturers regarding licensing.

If your product is something that you can be making and selling while you are working toward licensing, you will be establishing proof that there is a market for your product while you are replenishing your funds.

In November 1996, after receiving our Notice of Allowance, meaning that we were going to be awarded a patent from the USPTO, we licensed the patent and the trademark to a manufacturer for royalties. At the point of licensing, our licensee took over all financial responsibility for the three patents (two U.S. and one Canadian) and the trademark. Our licensee paid the issue fees and they have paid all maintenance fees in the intervening years. The patents and the trademark still belong to us, the inventors, but our licensee undertakes all financial responsibility for these legal documents. This Shoestring Budget™ invention was licensed with a nice advance payment against future royalties, and an annual guaranteed amount of royalty. At this writing, the **Ghostline®** brand is retailing over ten million dollars of product annually. This can happen to you!

What it takes to be a Shoestring Budget™ inventor

Shoestring Budget™ inventing is not easy, but inventing in general is not easy. To be a Shoestring Budget™ inventor you may have to be a little more patient than if you had lots of money to spend on your invention. You may have to settle for a less than perfect looking prototype. You can do this without diluting its effectiveness. You may have to do the work of obtaining your patent protection yourself. If you are willing to make the extra effort required to be a Shoestring Budget™ inventor and you have a great idea, you can succeed. It's all up to you, but this book will help you to get the most results for the amount of money that you have to spend. You will learn where you can cut down or completely eliminate some of the costs involved without sacrificing quality or protection for your intellectual property.

Ready to become a Shoestring Budget™ inventor? Let's get started!

CHAPTER TWO

Choose Your Best Idea!

Ideas, Ideas and more Ideas!

Every person who has had at least one idea for an invention has likely had multiple ideas for inventions. That is the way it seems to work for those creative individuals who constantly visualize easier, more convenient, more efficient, or more fun ways of interacting with the world around them. Talk to any inventor and he will tell you that his problem is not in coming up with a great idea, but because he has so many ideas, his problem comes in deciding which idea to pursue. This may sound like an inconsequential problem. You may think, "What a nice problem to have, too many great ideas," right? Wrong! It is one of the make or break points in the inventive process and it is an especially crucial stage for the inventor who is attempting to move a product to market on a shoestring budget. Careful selection of which idea to pursue may make the difference between the success and failure.

Keep a notebook in which you write down all of your ideas. If you don't write it down you may forget it until you see it on the shelf invented by someone else! Refer to your notebook and evaluate each idea and its potential when selecting the idea in which you will invest your time and your limited resources.

Ideas vs. Inventions

All too often first time inventors think of a product they would like to have themselves but it is completely out of their area of expertise, their range of experience or their skill sets to make it a reality. They don't know how to go about making it and they don't know who to go to in order to find out how to make it. We call these inventors "pie in the sky inventors." For example, not long ago a woman came to us who wanted to make a hand held device that could translate from one language to another (never mind that such products have been in existence for years!) She worked as a clerk in a department store and did not have any practical experience or educational background in electronic engineering. She did not understand, in the least, the circuitry and complex technology that would be required to develop such a product. What she had were drawings of how she thought the device might look. Her chances of getting her idea to market, if it weren't already on the market, were almost non-existent.

She made the mistake that many novice inventors make. She confused an idea with an invention. An idea is just that, an idea. An invention is a creation of a product or device that is developed as a result of study and experimentation. If you are inventing on a shoestring budget it is important to choose a project that you can actually do. Choose a simple yet useful product of which you can make a prototype. Dreaming up an invention that you do not have the ability to create is an exercise in frustration and futility.

 Don't jump to the conclusion that a product has not been invented because you have not seen it. Diligent research is required to determine whether a product has been patented or offered for sale.

Betty Nesmith Graham, a Dallas, Texas, typist is a perfect example of a first-time inventor who saw a simple solution to a common problem she faced each day. When she made errors in her typing, the erasing pencils that were in use at the time smeared and sometimes even tore or rubbed holes in the page. She thought, "There must be a better way" and Eureka!, it came to her! Being a person who enjoyed crafts and painting, she wondered, "What if you could paint over your typing mistakes the way you are able to paint over mistakes in art projects?" She set about developing a paint that would cover her typing mistakes and Liquid Paper was born!

So far, we have described someone who has an idea with no ability to see it through and someone who had an idea and developed a simple solution on her own, but there is a middle ground also. Take us, for example. We had the idea for a poster board with a "ghosted" grid but we did not know how to do it ourselves. Instead of saying, "Oh, well, we don't know how to do this," we took the third path. We had an idea for a simple product but we didn't know how to do it ourselves so we set about finding the people and resources who could teach us what we needed to know. We talked to a friend who was a retired printer. He told us we needed to learn about ink formulations and screen-printing. He directed us to a company called Ink, Inc. where they generously spent hours teaching us what we needed to know. We then went to a printer who was willing to try our many experiments. Weeks later after much trial and error we finally came up with the formulation and printing method that resulted in the "ghosted" grid that could be seen easily from a working distance but was virtually imperceptible from any distance away. This formulation is the basis of our three patents covering **Ghostline**® poster board. So, you see, if you have an invention that you don't know how to make but you are willing to do the required work to learn how to make it, you can still develop a successful invention.

 Sources of help are all around you. Ask friends and relatives for referrals for the type of help you need. Visit your nearest inventors club for networking and referrals that will save you time and money.

Will it be possible to protect your idea?

There are other criteria that you should also consider when determining whether you should pursue a particular idea. First, it is important to know whether you would be able to obtain strong legal protection for your idea. Companies that license patents from independent inventors insist on strong patent coverage before they are willing to commit to the product. Obviously, it would not be advantageous to a manufacturer to license a product on which there was no patent protection or weak patent protection. Their competitors could easily make the same or a similar product, thereby eliminating their advantage in the market place.

If your plan is to build a business around the product, rather than licensing it, you will see that it is equally important to make sure that the product can be protected. Just as a licensing manufacturer would insist on strong patent protection in order to achieve an advantage over his competitors in the marketplace before he would agree to license your invention, you would want the same advantage if you are the manufacturer. Choosing a product that has a great likelihood for obtaining patent protection is essential.

It is also important to understand that there are many great ideas for products that are simply not patentable. Perhaps they are ideas that are in the public domain. That is, they are owned by the public. These ideas may have had previous patent protection that has expired or they could be items that have been offered for sale in the marketplace without ever having had a patent. If they were ever patented, they may not be patented again, or if they have been offered for public sale, they may not be patented. Perhaps they are too similar to something that is currently protected by a patent. Perhaps they are not unique enough in design to receive a patent. There are a myriad of reasons why a product is not entitled to patent protection. Before you invest your time and your limited financial resources, it is important to determine whether patent protection is even an option.

You can determine this by performing both a market search and a patent search. Market and patent searches are discussed further in Chapter 4, IS IT YOURS TO PURSUE? After you have completed each of those searches, it is essential that you obtain a professional patent search including a legal opinion of patentability before you proceed. Only a qualified patent attorney or patent agent can assess the ultimate patentability of your product. Chapter 4 also offers tips for low cost professional patent searches as well as how you may visit with a patent attorney or patent agent about your idea for little or no cost.

Will your product have a large market?

The second criterion that you should consider when determining whether to pursue a particular idea is the market size for the potential product. Obviously, if there is a huge market for your invention, if millions and millions of people will want to buy your product, that is best. You may feel "in your gut" that the product will have a huge market but that is not good enough. Do the necessary research to find out exactly how large the potential market may or may not be. You may need to get U.S. Census Bureau figures or check the circulation figures for magazines or trade journals for the area of your invention. Your local reference librarian can help you to locate sales figures for similar or competing products in business directories. Or, a good, professional evaluation should help you to determine the potential market for your invention.

Don't assume just because you would like to have your invention that there is a large market for it. You may belong to the "Under 5' tall pastry chefs club" and have invented a short baster that is easier for a diminutive person to use. In other words, the product is helpful to you and a few of your fellow club members but there would not be a large market for it.

Are the benefits of your product easy to understand?

The third criterion is probably one you have not thought of but you can be sure that the manufacturers who might eventually license your product will be thinking of. You will have a much better chance of convincing a manufacturer to license your product if the benefits of your product are obvious. You may have a fantastic product but if the costs of educating the public on its benefits, why they need it and how it will make their lives easier, are too expensive, the manufacturer is likely to pass on your product no matter how terrific it is! If, on the other hand, the public will readily see the advantages of your product from its packaging or with minimal point of sale information, the manufacturer is much more likely to be interested in licensing it. If you plan to make and distribute the product yourself, it will be far less expensive and will involve less risk for you if it is something that consumers will immediately understand and desire without having to first be educated regarding the need it fills.

How expensive will it be to manufacture your product?

The fourth criterion that you must take into account is the cost of producing your item. Items that are inexpensive to produce are easier to license than expensive items since the monetary risk for the company is less with a low cost product. Ideally, the company to whom you would potentially license your invention would have everything they need to manufacture your product already in place. It would not require a lot of tooling up expenses for them. Obviously, to be inexpensive to produce, the cost of the manufacturing materials must be very low. If the raw materials are expensive, the product will not be inexpensive to produce. The cost of getting ready to manufacture your product, the tooling up cost, also goes into making a product inexpensive or expensive to produce. For example, if a plastic injection mold is required, that will greatly increase the initial cost of manufacturing your invention. Again, if you will be the manufacturer, it is no less important to have a product that will be inexpensive to produce. If you plan to manufacture your own product then look at the answers to all of these questions from the manufacturer's point of view as well as the inventor's point of view. In a manner of speaking, you are wearing both "hats" and you must view your product objectively and dispassionately in order to make a sound business decision on whether or not to pursue this particular idea.

We once spoke to a woman who had invented a specialized eye glasses lens that was helpful to people who suffered from a very rare eye condition. She perfected and patented her invention. She had a limited run made of her lenses because they were very expensive to produce, then she took them around to show them to ophthalmologists who treated this rare condition. The doctors were universally enthusiastic about having the product available for their patients. The ophthalmologists encouraged her to take the lens to manufacturers of eyeglasses lenses to see if they would make them commercially available. She was over the moon with excitement. The lens worked and the ophthalmologists loved it! She thought she had a sure thing. She was wrong. Her lenses were so expensive to produce that none of the lens manufacturers wanted to take them on. The cost of making the lens would cause the retail-selling price to be so high that it would be cost prohibitive for the consumer to purchase. Even though it was a great product, they would not license it because it did not allow for a profit to be made on the manufacturing, wholesale and retail levels of sales. It simply would not be a profitable product. These were obstacles this inventor was not able to overcome. If she had done her diligent research before embarking on this project, she would have seen the potential problems. She could have saved herself the costs of developing, prototyping, and patenting an invention that had no chance of success. You can see from this example that sometimes a really great product will not make it to the marketplace because it does not allow for enough profit.

Can the manufacturer make money on your product?

The fifth criterion for your consideration is, again, a concern for the manufacturer/licensee and thereby a concern for you also. Manufacturers have a formula for determining whether it will be cost efficient to manufacture a particular product. The manufacturing cost should be no more than 1/5 to 1/4 of the retail-selling price. If your product does not fit this formula your chances of finding a licensing partner are greatly reduced. What this means is if your product can be manufactured for $1 it should retail for at least $4-$5 or it is unlikely that you can license it.

Do not pull the suggested retail selling price for your product out of thin air. Don't base it on what your mother says she would be willing to pay for your product. You and your mother would probably pay more than any other person on earth for your product because you think it is such a great idea and your mother loves you. Too many inventors have an inflated opinion of what their product will sell for at retail. You will be exposed as an inexperienced product developer if you cannot make a logical argument for the price you suggest.

Is your product something that will be purchased again and again?

The sixth concern to evaluate before determining if you should move forward with your project is if your item is consumable. By that, we do not mean that it is something to eat. We mean that it is something that gets used up or needs to be purchased repeatedly. If your invention is something that is disposable, or is a one or two time use item, the same people will buy your product frequently. You can multiply the number of people who are likely to buy your product by the number of times they will need to replace it within a certain time period in order to estimate the market size. Manufacturers love products that consumers will buy again and again.

Will your product fit in with the manufacturer's product line?

Finally, if you can identify manufacturers who already have the distribution channels in place and your product would be a logical extension to their existing line of products, it will be a simple matter for them to add your product. In other words, these manufacturers already have shelf space in most or all of the retail outlets that would normally be expected to carry a product such as yours. The simpler it is for the manufacturers, the more likely they will be to give serious consideration to your product for licensing. Manufacturers like to license products for which they already have allotted shelf space in the stores. They can simply remove one of their slow selling existing products and replace it with your new, exciting and potentially good selling invention.

Some independent product developers (i.e. inventors) target specific manufacturers and deliberately develop products that fit into their existing product line. This helps to maximize the inventor's chances of success because he is staying within his "comfort zone" with products with which he is familiar.

The importance of matching your product to the manufacturer with the best "fit" for that product should not be underestimated. Your best chance of getting your product to market is in having it picked up by a company that already distributes similar products to the various retailers. Retailers almost never make the time to talk to an independent inventor with only one product and they will rarely, if ever, disrupt their planogram, or map of the store space, to make room for a one-product vendor. Getting your product with a manufacturer who already has the retailer's attention and shelf space solves these problems handily.

Our own personal story is the perfect example of this. While we were patent pending we manufactured and sold Ghostline® ourselves. We sold it to small office supply stores and teacher stores. That obviously was not our marketing goal at the same time, so we were also contacting all the large mass merchandising stores, such as Wal-Mart, K-Mart, Target, Kroger, Fred Meyer, etc., where we eventually wanted to see **Ghostline®** offered for sale. When we were able to get someone to talk to us, which was a rare event, we heard the same refrain over and over again. They all said, "We don't carry products from one-product vendors. Get your product with one of our distributors and we'll be happy to carry it." Most of the retailers would not talk to us at all because all of their buyers' time was taken up meeting with their regular distributors. It would have been much too time-consuming to meet with inventors of individual products.

Contact retail buyers in a professional manner if you choose to manufacture and distribute your product yourself. Do not attempt to get their attention with gifts or gadgets. This is a dead giveaway that you are an amateur and it will destroy your chances with them.

When we received the Notice of Allowance for our first patent, meaning that we would be awarded the patent, and were able to obtain a license agreement, that all changed. Our licensee was immediately able to place **Ghostline®** in all of the stores we had coveted, and more. Our new product had immediate nationwide distribution. If we had continued to manufacture and distribute the product ourselves, we would never have obtained that level of success.

The more of the above-listed criteria your invention meets, the greater are your chances of success. This does not mean that if it does not meet all of these criteria your product cannot be successful; it just means it is not as likely. For example, an expensive item that is a one-time purchase can be a successful invention if the potential market is large enough.

Inventors who are operating on a shoestring budget would be well advised to seriously consider each one of the listed criteria. Among your many great ideas, maximize your chances of success and minimize the likelihood that you will spend money unnecessarily by carefully choosing the idea that will require the least amount of cash outlay with the greatest potential for commercialization.

CHAPTER THREE

Bargains & Freebies!

Where to find free or nearly free help!

Independent inventors who are working on a shoestring budget often feel lost in an ocean of costly options. Every resource they find seems to carry a high price tag. Take heart! There are many free and nearly free resources available to the Shoestring Budget™ inventor if he will only take the time to locate them. In this chapter we will discuss several low cost resources that can help you through the inventive process.

Inventor Clubs

Inventor clubs can provide the resources, encouragement and contacts you will need as you move your product to market. The clubs are often populated with inventors who have successfully navigated the idea-to-market maze. They are willing to share their experiences and the expertise they have gained along the way. The knowledge the members of these organizations share can help you to avoid many of the pitfalls in inventing. It can also shorten the length of the process by teaching you the shortcuts they have learned. The inspiration club members offer can be as important as anything else can for keeping a new inventor motivated. Inventing is often discouraging, and just knowing a living, breathing person, not unlike yourself, who has invented successfully, can provide the encouragement you need to see you through the discouraging times.

Some of the successful inventors who belong to their local inventor support groups have licensed their products, others have chosen to build a business around their inventions, and still others have chosen countless other options such as catalog or infomercial sales for their products or patents. These individuals belong to the local inventor clubs because they wish to share their knowledge with others who are seeking success with their inventions.

Inventor groups often count patent attorneys, patent agents, prototype professionals, offshore manufacturing specialists and marketing specialists among their members. While it is true that all of these individuals undoubtedly belong to the groups in order to solicit business, it is also true that they give freely of their knowledge and expertise at the meetings. At an inventor group meeting you will have the opportunity to visit with these valuable resources.

Most inventor groups allow visitors to attend at least one meeting as a guest, free of charge. Membership fees are generally fairly low. Some groups only charge $10-$15 dollars per year for membership. The most expensive group we know of charges $125 for a lifetime membership. The average cost of membership is probably in the $30-$50 range. When you consider the contacts and resources you gain by joining an inventor group you will realize that the membership fee will be money well spent.

If you do not have a local inventor club, start one! **The United Inventors Association** *offers a book on how to start your own group. There are undoubtedly other independent inventors as well as intellectual property attorneys, patent agents and professionals of various types in your area who would welcome the establishment of such a group.*

We list all the inventor groups and clubs known to us in Appendix A of this book. If you have a club within driving distance, you should avail yourself of this low cost resource.

Inventor Shows and Workshops

Inventor shows and workshops occur in numerous cities across the country throughout the year. Many times there is no admission charge to go and browse through the exhibition hall where inventors have booths displaying their inventions. Just walking the hall and visiting with other inventors can be an extremely valuable source of information and contacts. Independent inventors are generally a very friendly and giving group of people who will gladly share their experiences and sources of help.

Inventor shows and seminars often have workshops and lectures on various phases of inventing taught by experts in the field. The fees to attend the educational sessions are usually quite nominal while the education you receive may save you thousands of dollars over the long haul. The two largest shows of this type are the **Yankee Invention Exposition**, which is held each October in Waterbury, Connecticut, and the **Minnesota Inventors Congress** which is held each June in Redwood Falls, Minnesota. Although these are the two largest such shows, others occur throughout the year.

 You can find a current list of upcoming inventor shows and programs through **Inventors' Digest Magazine** *at:*

www.inventorsdigest.com

or through the **United Inventors Association** *at:*

www.uiausa.org

The scam companies also hold inventor trade shows. Be certain that you are attending a legitimate one by checking its veracity on one of the above-mentioned websites.

Legitimate Websites for Inventors

The Internet provides many sources of legitimate help for the budget inventor. There are several websites and resources that are absolutely free. The first is the **United Inventors Association**, a non-profit organization that was formed in 1990 for the sole purpose of educating and providing resources for independent inventors. While there is a fee to actually join the UIA, there is a wealth of free information available to any visitor to their website, `www.uiausa.org`. They offer free articles about various stages and aspects of inventing, lists of resources, legislative updates affecting independent inventors, free newsletters, brochures, and products to help independent inventors, recommended books, and service providers. They offer advice on how to avoid the invention scam companies. Additionally, the UIA lists the legitimate inventor seminars and workshops that are scattered about the country. Many of these seminars and workshops, while not entirely free, are reasonably priced. Most of them allow visitors to peruse the booths manned by other inventors for no charge at all. The more networking you can do with other inventors, the better. You never know when another inventor you meet will have exactly the right information or know a person you should contact who will expedite the entire process for you.

 Discount coupons for three of the United Inventors' Association's most popular books are available in the back of this book.

In short, the United Inventors Association is an extremely valuable resource whether you choose to join the organization or not. Additionally, the inventor groups around the country are provided with free memberships in the UIA, so your membership in a local group will provide some UIA benefits.

 Beware of sites that offer a "free inventor's kit." This is one of the hallmark signs that it may be a scam company on the prowl for

unsuspecting independent inventors.

If you do not have a local inventor group in your area, the $97 fee for an individual membership in the UIA will allow you to submit questions that are answered by a board of experts. This is the next best thing to belonging to a local inventor club.

Another completely free Internet resource is our website:

www.asktheinventors.com

We offer a wealth of information on the steps of inventing, resources for independent inventors, news and events in the inventing world. In addition, thousands of independent inventors contact us each year with their individual questions. We personally answer each and every letter that we receive.

Patent Café [**www.patentcafe.com**] is another resource that provides a great deal of information for absolutely no charge. While it is true that they also have a variety of services for which there are charges, there are plenty of freebies too. Take advantage of them.

Inventors HQ [**www.inventorshq.com**] is yet another Internet site that offers free guidance and information for inventors on a budget. Randy Moyse, the man behind Inventors HQ, was once a shoestring budget inventor himself, having placed over thirty of his inventions into service with the U.S. Government. Located in Northwest Arkansas, near the international headquarters of one of the large mass market retailers, Randy has discovered an abbreviated method for submitting products to them. Using this method, he states that he can get you a response from Wal-Mart regarding their interest level in your product in ten days or less. You can contact Randy at: **inventorshq@earthlink.net.**

 Find a coupon for a $25 discount on his product submission service in the coupon section at the back of this book.

While there is a charge for a subscription to **Inventors' Digest Magazine,** their website is completely free. You can find articles relevant to issues faced by the independent inventor, classified ads for services needed by independent inventors as well as a complete listing of tradeshows for all sectors of the market. For very reasonable fees, usually around $1.50, you can order reprints of past articles that are particularly relevant to the category of your invention or your interest.

Inventors' Digest Magazine costs $35 for a yearly subscription but you can often avoid even that in a couple of ways. If you belong to an inventors group that is a member of the United Inventors Association you are entitled to a discount on your Inventors' Digest Magazine subscription, or you may look at the copies of the magazine that come to the group as a part of their membership. Many libraries across the country subscribe to Inventors' Digest Magazine. If your local library subscribes to Inventors Digest Magazine, you can check out copies of the magazine for no charge whatsoever. If your library does not subscribe, you may submit a request that they do so and they will often accommodate you. After all, their job is to meet the needs of their patrons.

You may find, after looking through an issue of Inventors Digest, that you want to subscribe in order to build your own library of these informative magazines. If you choose to subscribe to Inventors' Digest Magazine, you may order a regular subscription that will come to you in the mail or you may subscribe to the online version. The online version of Inventors' Digest Magazine is especially valuable to independent inventors since it allows you immediate access to current as well as past editions.

 Look on the coupon pages in the back of this book for a discount coupon on a subscription to Inventors Digest Magazine!

Libraries

We all owe a debt of gratitude to Benjamin Franklin, revolutionary, founding father, international diplomat, printer, inventor, and scientist for being one of the establishers of the first public library in this country. Public libraries are an incredible resource for independent inventors on a shoestring budget. Your local neighborhood library offers an abundance of information that can save you time and money. These libraries often have books, audio, and video materials that explain everything from how to make a prototype to how to license your great idea and everything in between.

The library's resource or business department has books such as the **Thomas Register** and **Dun and Bradstreet's Million Dollar Companies.** The Thomas Register is a set of twenty books that lists most American manufacturers according to the types of products they manufacture. It also lists important contact information for the officers and departments of the companies. A limited version of the Thomas Register is available online at:

www.thomasnet.com

D & B's Million Dollar Companies is another valuable resource when it is time to locate potential licensees. The business department of your local library will also have hundreds of directories of manufacturers for specific industries.

If you choose to license your product, you can often find every major manufacturer of your category of invention in those directories. If, instead, you choose to manufacture your product yourself, these directories often list distributors and sales representatives who work in your sector of the market. Either direction you choose to go, the trade directories are an extremely valuable free resource of information in one neat, tidy location. They can literally save you hours or days of time spent attempting to locate your potential customer, a manufacturer who might be interested in licensing your invention.

With the advent of the Internet, the information you are able to access through your local library expanded exponentially. Now, if a book on a particular subject is available at any library, it is available to you. You simply submit a request and the library will have the book sent to your local library for you to pick up. Inter-library loans are now quite common.

 Libraries now have large collections of "how-to" videos. Check it out! You may find instructions on how do the very things you need. For example, they may have videos that show you how to make plastic molds, or how to solder, etc.

Most university and college libraries are also open to the public. You may, or may not, be allowed to check out books, but you certainly have the opportunity to look at their collection of books, magazines and journals and glean information from them while you are at the library. University libraries are often the repositories of technical journals and books that are not available through the public library system. If your invention is technical or has technical components, you may find the exact information you seek at your local university or college library.

Scattered across the country are approximately sixty **Patent and Trademark Depository Libraries**. Patent and Trademark Depository Libraries (PTDL's) are housed within existing public, academic, state and research libraries. The librarians who work in the PTDL's are specially trained by the United States Patent and Trademark Office and can help inventors perform patent and trademark searches using the printed Gazettes of issued patents as well as the latest computer programs and technology for patent and trademark searching. PTDL's have all the listings for patents and trademarks that are found in the USPTO's Virginia offices. There is no difference. This means that you can accomplish as thorough and complete a patent search at one of these PTDL's as you can accomplish at the USPTO in Virginia.

Independent inventors should not rely on the results of any patent search they perform at a PTDL without the guidance and assistance of the PTDL librarians. The librarians offer their help as a part of their duties. Take advantage of their expertise.

In addition to being able to perform patent and trademark searches, the libraries often provide seminars, talks and sessions with local patent professionals. Check with your closest PTDL to find out when the next free session is scheduled.

PTDL's are a tremendous local resource for businesses and independent inventors alike. Since any library must provide free public access in order to be classified as a PTDL, you can feel comfortable and welcome at any library that includes a PTDL whether it is a public library, private academic library, a state library or a research library.

United States Patent & Trademark Office

The **United States Patent & Trademark Office** is also a free resource which offers many valuable programs and opportunities for inventors on a shoestring budget. They frequently have free online sessions with patent examiners and patent attorneys. At these online sessions these professionals answer questions submitted by the public. These sessions occur with some regularity on a monthly or bimonthly basis. You can find when the next session is scheduled on the **USPTO website** at:

www.uspto.gov

or through your local PTDL. If you are not able to login to the actual session, the transcripts of the questions and answers are available on the USPTO's website. If you have an attorney handling the prosecution of your patent application, this may be your only opportunity to visit with an actual examiner and ask a general question. Obviously, during these sessions they are not able to answer questions relating directly to your patent application.

The USPTO website also has an extensive list of frequently asked questions. You may find the answer to a question there and save yourself the time and money of consulting a patent attorney or patent agent. News of pending and proposed changes to patent and trademark law, forms for use in filing patents and trademarks, lists of patent attorneys and patent agents as well as ways to check on the status of your patent application can all be found on the USPTO website.

Schools, Colleges and Universities

Many inventors overlook free or nearly free resources that are right under their noses: nearby schools and universities. Schools have marketing and business departments and they are constantly on the lookout for projects in which to involve the students.

The marketing department of a nearby university can be an extremely valuable yet inexpensive resource for inventors on a shoestring budget. Professors often jump at the opportunity to involve the students in research for an actual product that is in development. Many times it becomes a semester assignment for the students to do a thorough market search and evaluation of the potential viability of a product. This often includes the students conducting visits to local stores, thorough internet searches and catalog searches. The work done by the students is often more thorough than the work done by the independent inventor simply because many students are involved in the project.

 Do not assume that a thorough market search will replace a patent search. It will not. Many items are patented that never make it to the marketplace.

Before you approach a college professor to ask him to take on your product as a class project you will need to clearly establish what it is you wish to learn. There are usually no set guidelines on what the students will and will not do as a part of the project. The clearer you can be with your objectives, the more valuable their research will be to you. It is common for their studies to include research on the cost of manufacturing your product, possible channels of distribution, competing products, market resistance, advertising or consumer education that would be required for the end users to see the value of your product, potential retail pricing, and surveys and focus groups to study market acceptance for your product. The students may even be able to locate manufacturers that might eventually be interested in licensing your product. They may also research the viability of building a business around your invention. If your product is selected as a class project you could receive thousands of dollars worth of research absolutely free!

Using your product as a class project is a serious commitment on the professor's part. You will need to approach it in a businesslike manner and be prepared with a list of what you hope to gain from the project. If you go with unclear objectives the professor is not likely to take you or your project seriously.

Assuming the results are favorable, the report you receive at the conclusion of the project can be an important and compelling part of the eventual product presentation that you will prepare for either attracting a potential licensee or obtaining funding for your start up business.

You are undoubtedly saying to yourself, "This all sounds great, but what is the catch?" You are right. There is a catch. Class projects usually take an entire semester to complete. If you are in a hurry to get the results of a marketability study then you will have to pay for the quick results by hiring one of the legitimate professional firms that perform this service. If, on the other hand, you are trying to save every penny possible, it may be worth it to you to wait a semester for the results. It's your call.

Colleges and universities are not the only sources of free marketability studies. High schools all over the country are starting entrepreneurial programs for their students. Often these programs are willing and anxious to perform market studies, surveys and focus groups for new products.

Contact your local school district to see if they offer an entrepreneurial program. Get the name or names of the faculty members in charge. Explain your product and your needs. Again, the more precise you can be in what you are requesting, the more likely it will be that you will receive usable data.

 If you have a choice, choose a college or university program over a high school program. The maturity level, academic background, and the life experience level of the college age student will usually result in a more valuable report.

Vocational Schools

Local vocational schools can be particularly helpful in the development and prototyping phase of the inventive process. There are vocational schools for virtually every trade imaginable, from electronics and computers to welding and automotive repair. Students work under the close supervision of their instructors. You can often get a prototype, or a particular part of a prototype, made by a vocational school for a fraction of the cost a regular shop would charge for the same work.

These schools can be a low cost source of help during the research and development phase of your invention. You will need to work closely with them and, of course, have them sign the contractor's non-disclosure agreement beforehand.

Small Business Development Centers

Scattered across the country are more than 900 Small Business Development Centers. These offices are usually affiliated with community colleges. The sole purpose of the SBDC is to assist small business owners. They offer many free services and classes on a variety of subjects that will maximize the chances that your small business will succeed in the marketplace. Free counseling with business consultants who will help you to set goals and even to develop your personalized business plan is available for the asking. Some Small Business Development Centers even offer business incubation for a nominal cost. Business incubation will allow you to share an office, office equipment and even secretarial assistance with other start-up companies in office space provided by the SBDC. If you are building a business around your invention, taking advantage of the business incubation services offered by the SBDC will allow you to save substantial amounts of initial cash outlay when your income is likely to be at its lowest.

Small Business Development Centers can also provide information and guidance on how to apply for and obtain Small Business Administration loans through your local bank or credit union.

Service Corps of Retired Executives (SCORE)

In many communities across the country there are local branches of the Service Corps of Retired Executives (SCORE). This organization is a completely free mentoring program that is made up of retired executives who succeeded in their careers and who are now willing to share their knowledge and expertise, absolutely free of charge, with those who are attempting to follow in their footsteps. Each SCORE office is as different as the individuals who make it up. You may find the exact person who can answer your questions, give you direction and save you from making costly mistakes. Utilize their generosity. To locate your nearest SCORE facility, go into a search engine such as Google, and type SCORE. This will bring up a number of links to guide you to your local office.

The Buddy System

One other option you might consider for getting some help in all areas of your invention is to have a partner involved so that you are not entirely alone with the process. This is not feasible for every independent inventor, but if you have someone in whom you have total trust, who is equally excited about the idea, and who is willing to be fully involved in every area, this can advance your cause in so many ways.

In our situation with **Ghostline®**, we found that with two of us handling the tasks, we got them done at a faster rate. It also was helpful to have two minds looking at the problems and challenges, not to mention sharing the expenses equally. Of course, if you do this you will be sharing ownership of the patent and settling for one-half of the profits. But, it may be important to you to have the security of someone else who is as passionate as you are about getting the product on the market and who can help in all aspects of accomplishing the task. And, since inventing and marketing a new product is fun, but not particularly easy or fast, having a buddy gives you a comrade with whom to share the excitement and it may increase your chances of success.

As you can see, there are many resources available for the inventor on a shoestring budget if he will only seek them out and take full advantage of them. Whenever you are feeling alone in the process, refer back to this chapter and reach out for the help that is there for you for little or no cost.

CHAPTER FOUR

Your Idea:
Is It Yours To Pursue?

Are you the first with this idea?

In the first flush of a new idea, it is sometimes difficult to think that anyone might have ever thought of the idea before. When that eureka moment hits you, it seems like your own singular moment of pure inspiration and the ingenious solution to a problem. It could well be exactly that. However, since ideas are in the ether, and thus they occur to many people and often at around the same time, it is important to make certain that the idea is really yours to pursue before you spend a lot of time and some of your hard-earned money in its pursuit.

Don't assume that a product is not on a store shelf simply because you never thought to look for it. We once heard of a woman who paid for a visit with a patent attorney to discuss her great idea for a pre-packaged moist towelette made for cleaning eyeglasses. Then, on a subsequent visit to her local drugstore, she saw that product on the shelf with the other eye products! She made the mistake of assuming that it was a brand new idea without even doing a preliminary search at her local drugstore!

Market search

Your early market search and preliminary patent search are both types of research for which the only cost is some of your time and they are important educational phases in the development of your invention. Your first step will be to check out every store in your local area where such an item as you envision might be offered for sale. If, for example, your idea is for a new type of kitchen gadget, you will certainly want to check the kitchen specialty stores. But, you will also want to check any and every store that sells kitchen gadgets. This means that you might find yourself looking in stores such as Wal-Mart, Target, your local grocery store, the hardware store, the corner convenience store, the department stores at the mall and even the stores that specialize in unusual items, such as Brookstone or Sharper Image. You will need to be creative in thinking of all of the places where an item such as the one you envision might be offered for sale.

While you are making the rounds of the stores looking at the similar products, this is an opportunity for you to do some other research that will get you ahead of the game when you are ready to market your invention. Take a small pad and a pen with you and write down the name and location of the manufacturers of similar merchandise. You will find this information on all products that are offered for sale. It will be on a sticker or a hangtag or stamped somewhere on the item. These are the companies that will be your marketing targets later if you plan to license your product for royalties. Or, they will be your competition if you plan to build a business around your invention. Either way, it will be to your advantage to know as much as you can about these companies that manufacture products similar to your invention.

If your invention is something that is not specifically a retail item, such as a medical invention that would be sold through specialty outlets, you will need to track down those specific outlets and catalogs (perhaps with the help of a medical professional) in order to search in that area. However, if you have developed such an invention, chances are excellent that you are already familiar with those specialized outlets.

If your invention is in a field that is a specialized area in which the products are not found in the usual retail outlets, you may need assistance from professionals in that industry during your research or development phase. Be sure to have each person who assists you to sign a non-disclosure document for your files.

Once you have searched the stores in your area as thoroughly as you possibly can and have convinced yourself that your idea is not currently being offered in the local stores, it is time to get online and begin an Internet market search. There are a couple of steps to be completed in this search in order to be thorough here and it will be a bit time-consuming, but it is not difficult. You will do a key word search and a catalog search.

You will start your Internet search by making a list of key words that might be used to describe your invention. You will be searching through the links to see what products similar to your invention are being offered for sale on the Internet. Even if you feel strongly that no similar products exist, you will be surprised by what a key word search will turn up. Use the most descriptive words you can think of and get as specific as possible in the description. By this, we mean get right down to the most common descriptive words for your invention. For example, if your product is a kitchen gadget, it is far too broad to simply type in, "Kitchen Gadget." This would bring up many more links than you would want, or need, to search. If the invention is designed for peeling grapes, say so. Type in, "Grape Peeler." Then, as you begin to click on and follow the links that this brings up, you will find more words on those pages that will help you to reach even more links and get even more specific. For example, you may find words that are specific to that type of product – i.e. rind removal – that would lead you to entirely new links to explore.

Here, you will find a cornucopia of places where products in the category you are searching are being sold. The same stores that you have just visited will likely have links on the Internet. So, why bother to go out to the stores in the first place? Because you want to actually see the similar products that are on store shelves. And, you want to gather the information that you can get from the product labels. If you should find a product that is offered for the same purpose as your idea, you can inspect it closely to see if your idea is an improvement on that product. Also, retailers do not usually have every product that is in their stores on their websites, so it is important to make sure that you do not overlook something by failing to make that trip to the store.

Individuals often make and sell products on the Internet that are offered nowhere else. If you neglect to do a good Internet search, you will miss this prior art. What is prior art?

- If an active patent covers a product, you cannot legally make and sell it.

- If that patent has expired, that product is said to be in the public domain and is now available to anyone to make and sell.

- A product that has never been patented but has been offered for sale to the public is also said to be in the public domain and can never be patented.

All of the above examples are prior art; products that have already been presented to the public and cannot now be patent protected. One of the first things the examiners at the patent office will do when they begin with your application is to initiate a thorough search for prior art. If you failed to find these products but they were found in subsequent searches related to your patenting efforts, your patent would be rejected and you would have spent your money and your time in vain. It pays to be meticulous in your Internet searching.

Once you have followed the links from your key word search and satisfied yourself that your invention is not being sold through those links, it is time to do a catalog search. This can also be done on the Internet. Most all, if not all, of the catalogs are on the Internet today and there are several ways to find them. You can go into the search engines and type in "Catalogs," and this will bring up lots of links for multiple catalogs. To be sure that you don't overlook any of them, be sure to also check the alternate spelling, "catalogue," as some of them use the British spelling. Most catalogs have a search option, allowing you to type in key words. This can help to expedite your search.

Preliminary patent search

If you have done your store and Internet market searches carefully and you have not found your invention, that is an excellent start! Chances are pretty good that your product is not currently being sold. However, you still have a couple of hurdles to get over before you can breathe easily that your idea really belongs to you. According to the United States Patent and Trademark Office (USPTO), over 97% of the patents that are issued to independent inventors never make it to the marketplace! We will talk about this grim statistic in a later chapter and how you can avoid being a part of it. But, what this statistic means is that the patent database is full of patents that have never been seen on store shelves. You will need to make sure that your idea is not one of those that have been patented already.

The United States patent database is huge and complicated, and it would be foolhardy for novice inventors to believe that they could do thorough enough searches to base utility patent applications on them. But, with a little bit of instruction in how to get around on the USPTO website, anyone can do a pretty good preliminary search. What we mean by a preliminary search is this: if you go into the USPTO database and, with a limited amount of searching, you find your invention idea staring back at you; it is time to reassess your idea. Is the prior art (patent) that you just found your exact idea? If it is not, is your idea an improvement over that product? If you believe it to be your exact idea, it is probably best to set it aside and move on to your next idea before you spend any more time or any money on it. But, if you think your idea is significantly different or better, print that patent and take it to a patent agent or attorney for a legal opinion.

If you find a patent that appears to be your exact idea, be sure to read the claims section carefully to make sure that it truly is identical before you abandon your dream. Sometimes two products can be made for the exact same purpose and they can look very similar or even identical in patent drawings and still be very different in the embodiments of how they are actually made.

The steps given below are very basic and they are not intended to be exhaustive but they will help you to learn how to do a simple, preliminary patent search in order to avoid unnecessarily spending money for a professional patent search if you should happen upon your invention idea very quickly.

The USPTO database is the same one that you would find if you went to one of the patent and trademark depository libraries that are scattered around the country. By the way, although you can do these searches on your home computer, it is a good idea to go at least once to one of these libraries if you have the opportunity to do so because the librarians are so knowledgeable and helpful and it is a wonderful experience for an inventor. It's just a great place for creative people to hang out and learn!

The United States Patent and Trademark Depository Libraries around the country frequently hold free classes and seminars on all subjects related to inventing, patents and trademarks. Call your nearest branch to be placed on a mailing list for these opportunities.

The website for the **United States Patent and Trademark Office** is:

www.uspto.gov

Although we are discussing patent searching here, you will find that this website offers a great deal more than that and you will likely find yourself going back there again and again for the wealth of information that you can find there. The database for trademarks is also on this website. Additionally, you will find a glossary of terms related to patents and trademarks and information on just about every area of intellectual property, as well as fee schedules, inventor resources, depository library locations and a roster of all of the patent attorneys and agents who are licensed to practice before them. Although copyrights are not handled by the USPTO, you will also find a link on their website for the Library of Congress Copyright Office.

 Watch the USPTO website homepage for notices of free online live chats with examiners and other intellectual property experts. This is your chance to get your questions answered in real time right from the patent office… a wonderful freebie!

Comprehensive patent searches, such as the ones performed by professional patent search firms, are a bit like peeling an onion, layer by layer. The USPTO database is a compilation of millions of patents and they are cataloged in a number of ways. Each patent is assigned a number, of course, but they are also listed in classes and sub-classes according to categories. Each classification or sub-classification will lead to more and more patents to inspect. We are told that patent searches don't actually have a specific point at which they are concluded; the searchers simply search until they feel that they have examined all of the relevant prior art.

*If you are searching from your home computer, the first thing you will need to do is make sure that you have plug-in software for viewing TIFF images. There is very specific TIFF plug-in software that you must use in order to view the full-page patent images and the good news is that it is free! Simply follow one of these links and download it: **AlternaTIFF** [www.alternatiff.com] or InterneTIFF [www.internetiff.com].*

The USPTO offers a seven-step searching strategy that you can use if you wish to begin your search by finding the classification numbers. The instructions for doing that search can be found on their website at:

www.uspto.gov/web/offices/ac/ido/ptdl/step7.htm

If you prefer to use the quick search method and begin with a key word search, you will find a free step-by-step guide to doing that type of search at:

asktheinventors.com/Books/patentsearch.htm

This is the type of search that we will discuss here and, again, we stress that this is a cursory search only, not to be considered a reliable enough search on which to base a patent application. It may be helpful to you if it saves you the money you might spend for a professional search if your invention idea is quickly found there.

Even though this is called a "Quick Search," there is no such thing as a really quick patent search if you are to be thorough. If you are looking for a specific patent and you have information such as the patent number or the inventor's name, then it is indeed quick. But, if you are looking for any and all prior art that could be relevant to your idea, be prepared to spend some time in your search. Periodically, the USPTO makes changes in the appearance of their website's homepage and in some of the basic ways of navigating the site. These instructions are functional at the time this book is being written.

The search that we outline here is composed of searching the database in four ways:

1. Key Word
2. Classification
3. Prior Art (listed on individual patents)
4. Hybrid (using classification and key word)

Key Word

Begin by going to the USPTO website [**www.uspto.gov**]. On the left side of the homepage, click on "Patents". On the left side of this page, click on "Search." Again on the left side of the next page, under "Issued Patents", click on "Quick Search." This will open a page with spaces for two terms, each with a choice of fields for that term. There are many options for ways to search here and we will suggest only one of those options at this point.

Using words that might be used to describe your invention, fill in the blank for Term 1. You may use more than one word in each blank if you wish, such as "ballpoint pen." Although you could go over and select a specific field for that term in Field 1, we suggest that you leave it set at, "All Fields." This way, your search will look for that term anywhere that it might appear in the entire patent. Next, to narrow your search a bit more, if the ballpoint pen you are searching for is made from a ceramic material, you might type "ceramic" in Field 2 and again leave Field 2 set on "All Fields" in order to seek that word in the entire patent.

"Select Years", the field in which to select the time period for your search, is preset on "1976 to Present." Even though the entire patent database is available to you, beginning with the year 1790, only those from 1976 forward are available by this search method. You will need the patent numbers in order to access patents issued before 1976. We will tell you how to find those a bit further into the searching process. Even if you select the choice, "1790 to present" (entire database), your search at this point will only include patents from 1976 forward when you are searching with key words.

Once you have filled in the blanks for Term 1 and Term 2 , click on "Search." This will bring up a page telling you how many patents have been found that include those terms and you may scroll down and read the titles of those patents. These are actual links that you may click on to view the patents. You will find patents listed there that have no connection whatever to what you are searching for and you may wonder how they got on the list. They got there because those key words that you selected appear somewhere in those patents.

Begin scrolling down the links and click on each patent that looks as if it could possibly be similar to your idea. Familiarize yourself with the layout of a patent. You will see that on the first page there is a great deal of information: the patent number, date of issue, inventor's name, the abstract (a brief statement of the technical disclosure including that which is new in the art to which the invention pertains), if the patent has been assigned and to whom, if foreign patent applications have been filed, the classification numbers, references cited (prior art) , if an attorney or agent was used and if so, who they are, the claims, a description of the invention including the background art in the field (this is where the problem is described that the invention addresses), and the disclosure of the invention (how the invention solves the problem). Also, at the top and bottom of the page you will find a group of links to help you navigate around the database, including one to click on in order to view the patent drawings.

Each patent that appears to be similar to your idea will bear some closer examination. You will want to make a note of the patent number and then take a look at the patent images to see if it looks at all like your idea. If it is at all similar to your invention, print the first page because you will need the information there for the other parts of your search. We suggest that you print the entire patent including images if it is really close to your idea.

You will repeat these steps with as many key words as you can think of to describe your idea. As you read through some of the patents you will come across other words to try.

Maybe you didn't find anything that seemed that similar to your invention. In that case, you will begin examining the patents on items that have been invented for the same purpose as your invention. All patents have some prior art shown, even if it is not the same type of item. Look for inventions that address the same problem your invention addresses.

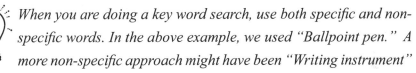 *When you are doing a key word search, use both specific and non-specific words. In the above example, we used "Ballpoint pen." A more non-specific approach might have been "Writing instrument" because it would have brought up patents for other types of pens that could possibly bear upon the patentability of your pen. These patents might not have shown up on this search using specific words only.*

Classification

After you have done key word searches using all of the appropriate key words you can think of, it is time for a classification search. Using the patents you have found that are most similar to your invention or that address the same problem, write down the classification numbers. You should start seeing the same numbers appearing repeatedly. This is of course because you are narrowing down your search to the classifications into which your invention falls. You should have several classification numbers. Each classification number appears as a set of numbers followed by a forward slash and a second set of numbers.

Go back to the "Quick Search" screen and enter one of these numbers in the "Term 1" blank and in the field opposite that blank, on the pull-down screen, select "Current US Classification." Click on "Search." You are likely to find again that many of the patents are not similar to yours at all so just look closely and pull up for examination any that appear similar. You will do the same thing with these patents that you did during the key word search. That is, you will print the first page of anything slightly similar and the entire patent including images if it appears to be really similar to your idea.

Prior Art

Using the patents that are most similar to your invention, click on the link for each patent that is listed under "References Cited." This is the prior art that has been listed as being the most similar to that patent. This is where you will find the patents that are similar, regardless of when they were issued. Often you will find patents dating back many years in this section. Examine each of those carefully, looking at the images if you need to, in order to understand how they are similar or dissimilar to your idea. If you continue to pursue your invention and a patent application is filed, some of these same patents may be cited as prior art on your application. Look at the classification numbers on these patents to make sure that you have not missed one that should be checked.

Hybrid

This search is exactly what it sounds like, a cross-search between key words and classification numbers. Here, you will take the classification numbers that you have narrowed down to in your search (and there may be quite a few of them) and return to the "Quick Search" screen. This time, you will place one of the classification numbers you have isolated into the first search term blank and select "Current US Classification" from the pull down list to place in the opposite field. Then, in the second search blank, Term 2, you will place one of your key words or phrases and again select "All fields." This will narrow your search even further.

You will continue in this manner until you feel that you have located every issued patent that could possibly influence the patentability of your invention. Then, you will need to return to the "Quick Search" screen and repeat the process all over again with the right side of that screen, the Published Applications. These are applications that have been published but not granted. Many, but not all, patent applications are published eighteen months after filing and you can access those. If the applicant has specifically requested that his application not be published and he is applying only for a U.S. patent, his application will remain secret until the patent issues.

These instructions are much abbreviated and if you feel that you want more detailed instructions, including graphics, please print the free patent searching guide from our website at:

www.asktheinventors.com/books/patentsearch.htm

This patent searching guide was written before the most recent changes to the USPTO website, so you may find slight changes, but the information in this guide is still valid and you may find it helpful.

When you have completed these steps, you may feel that you have done a thorough search and are now ready to file your patent application. Think again! Even the most thorough search done by an independent inventor is likely to overlook something that will be found by a professional search. Your preliminary search should never take the place of a professional search. It is only intended to save you from paying for a professional search if your invention is very easy to find. The idea here is to safeguard your inventing dollars.

A professional search is still a good use of your inventing dollars. While professional search firms use the same USPTO database that is available to you, they have very expensive specialized software that facilitates their search progress to make it far more thorough and comprehensive than the search that most individuals can do for themselves.

If you have isolated patents that are a concern to you, it is time to take that information to a patent agent or a patent attorney for a professional opinion. Many patent attorneys do not charge for your first visit with them in order to help you determine if you should apply for a patent. Call and ask if that is the policy before making the appointment. This could save you several hundred dollars!

Although patent searching is time-consuming, the USPTO database is free to you and the above-mentioned systematic patent searching guide is also free. Simply print it and use it. You don't even have to download it. So, you can see that your invention will take an investment of your time, but the market searching and preliminary patent searching steps will cost you nothing.

One last thought . . . if you have an idea for a product that you have yearned to bring to market, and you have not found it on the market but you have found a patent that stands in your way . . . there may be a Shoestring Budget™ solution for you. The patent you found may be one of those many that are just languishing on the patent database, never having been brought to market. You could be the answer to that patent holder's prayer!

All patents have information right on their front page regarding the inventor and his location as well as information on the attorney or agent who handled the patent for him. It is not difficult to track down patent holders. You may be able to work out a partnership arrangement to bring the product to market that would benefit both of you. Or, he may be willing to sell his patent to you for a price that is far less than it would have cost you to file for and get the patent. This could be a good option if your product idea has been patented but not marketed. You won't know unless you try!

CHAPTER FIVE

Document Your Idea & Start Protecting It.

Early Protective Measures

Of all of the steps involved in developing and marketing a new idea, probably the most financially intimidating are those steps that are connected to protecting your invention to make sure that it belongs to you. The subject of patents, especially, can be frightening because for the novice inventor there is so much of the unknown involved regarding the legal costs.

We agree that it is frightening, particularly when we read or hear about patents requiring years to obtain and running up thousands of dollars in legal costs. We will discuss some cost-cutting methods for obtaining patent protection in Chapter 9, but first you need to understand the protection measures you will need to take long before you are even ready to file for that patent.

From the moment that great idea occurs to you, the paranoia sets in. It suddenly feels as if you need to maintain total secrecy in order to keep others from stealing your great idea. Right? This is a normal and even a prudent attitude for all inventors, both the novice and the seasoned inventor. After all, how many times have you had an idea, failed to follow through and

47

then seen your great idea sitting on the store shelves, invented by someone else?

This has happened to most of us at one time or another. It's a sinking feeling when that happens to you because you realize that it could have been your invention. It should also reinforce for you what good ideas you have! Let your next good idea be your home run by taking early steps to protect the idea and then following through with the invention.

Make a Paper Trail

Many of the early protective measures for your invention idea are so inexpensive that anyone can do them without even making a dent in the budget. Here, we will go through each of these steps, why they are important (even vital!) and how to do them.

Poor Man's Patent?

Before we start, the first thing we want to do is to debunk a method that has been around for years and is still practiced and believed in by the uninitiated inventor. We are speaking of the practice that has been referred to as the "poor man's patent". It involves writing the idea down, placing it into an envelope and mailing it to yourself. The theory here is that you would have your idea sealed inside an envelope bearing a postmark, thereby proving the date you first conceived your invention. It sounds like a good idea, doesn't it? It is worthless for legally proving when you first had your good idea! This practice was actually tested in court and the ruling was that it is ineffective because a person could simply mail an unsealed envelope to himself and then add the information at a later date!

Now that we know what doesn't work, let's get ready to set your real protection in place. There are several things you will probably do when that great idea first occurs to you. You will likely develop a crude prototype if your idea is simple enough and if your prototype can be developed quickly and inexpensively enough to prove that your theory is viable. And, you will probably start searching stores and perhaps the Internet to make sure that your idea hasn't already been invented by someone else. These are good first steps.

 Sending a detailed description of your invention to friends, associates or even sources of help via e-mail is a bad idea. The Internet is not secure and your e-mail could conceivably be intercepted.

Inventor's Journal

Another important early step is to begin immediately to write everything about your idea in an inventor's journal. Your inventor's journal will be a continuous record of your invention from the time you first conceived the idea all the way through the research, development, protection and marketing phases. You will describe the idea, how you happened to come up with it, the research you did, the prototyping experimentation, and so on.

Your Inventor's Journal will be a diary of your invention that includes every little detail. Think of it as being almost like a baby book with your invention being the baby. You will record the birth of the idea, and each step along the way as it develops into a full-grown invention.

Include in your journal the things you tried that didn't work, what did work, the products you came across that were similar to your idea, the people you consulted for help and their contribution to the effort, cost of materials, etc. In other words, everything about your experience should be recorded. You can even staple the receipts for prototyping materials right to the pages if you wish.

Why is it important to keep an inventor's journal? If all goes well with the development, protection and marketing of your invention and that is

49

the goal, your journal will only be something for you to look back on and reminisce. However, if, God forbid, your eventual patent is ever challenged or you need to challenge someone else's patent, your journal becomes a legal document, proving exactly when you began working on your invention and that you worked on it continuously without large time gaps during which no work was being done.

Patents that are pending are not published until they have been pending for eighteen months and, even then, some pending patents are not published. This means that you will have no way of knowing if someone else has filed for a patent on your same idea.

The United States and Canada are First to Invent countries, rather than First to File countries, as is the case with the rest of the world. This means that even if someone else has filed for a patent on your same invention before you filed, if you can prove that you were working on the idea at an earlier date than the other inventor, you can be awarded the patent. This is why your inventor's journal can be so important to you.

What exactly is an inventor's journal and where do you get one? Your inventor's journal, sometimes referred to as a lab notebook, can be simply an inexpensive composition book. These little books are readily available in office supply stores, drug stores and even grocery stores. You will find them in the school supply department and they often have a black, marbleized cover. They have lined pages and they sell for around two or three dollars, often even less. The pages should also be numbered, so if the book you buy is not numbered, go ahead and number the pages yourself.

Because your journal could conceivably end up in court as a legal document, there are specific rules for how the journal must be kept in order to leave no room for questions about the when, where, how, etc. of your invention.

1. **It must have the pages stitched into the backing, not pasted in.**

Obviously, a loose-leaf notebook could have pages easily added or removed without detection. So that type of notebook is unacceptable. Spiral notebooks and those with pages pasted in can have pages removed without detection. These are also unacceptable. A journal that has pages that are stitched into it cannot have pages added and it is very difficult to remove them without leaving tell-tale signs. For reasons that are by now obvious, computer files are also completely unacceptable as an inventor's journal.

2. **Handwrite your journal in a particular way.**

This may be the only time when you will ever be advised to write all over a page, ignoring margins. But, that is exactly how you will create your inventor's journal. You will begin writing at the very top of each page and write from top to bottom and from side edge to side edge, completely ignoring the margins. If you need to leave space for some reason, draw an x through that space, indicating the space is purposely left blank.

If you make a mistake and want it noted that the information should not be a part of your journal, draw a *single line* through the part that is to be ignored. *Never erase or cover up anything.* This could indicate in a legal proceeding that you had something to hide. Full disclosure is all-important if you have to defend your invention in court.

Some inventors seem to consider a hand written inventor's journal to be from the Stone Age and choose instead to keep their journals on their computers. This is a mistake. A computer version of your inventor's journal would NOT be considered a legal document. The hand written version may be a little time consuming but if you ever have to go to court, the time will have been well spent.

3. **Have your journal witnessed.**

Occasionally, perhaps once every few weeks, get a friend or acquaintance that you trust (but not a close family member) to read, date and sign the information as a witness. You can just write, "Read and witnessed by:" and have him to sign his name and date it on each occasion. Some people go so far as to have it notarized but that is probably not necessary. Most people who place their notary seals on documents are only notarizing the signatures anyway, rather than the information in the document.

The witness who signs your journal does not have to be the same person each time. You may use the same witness, or not. The important thing is to get each person who witnesses your journal to sign a non-disclosure agreement for your files. If you use the same witness more than once, you will not need a new non-disclosure agreement (NDA) each time.

Non-disclosure Agreements

The non-disclosure agreement will become a familiar document that you are likely to use repeatedly until your legal intellectual property protection is obtained. This, too, is a legal document, but it is one that you can easily obtain and use without cost and without the assistance of an attorney.

What is a non-disclosure agreement? This document, also called a confidentiality agreement, is a simple document that states that the inventor has disclosed his invention idea to another person and that the recipient of the information agrees to hold the information confidential. These documents, usually written by attorneys but widely available without consulting an attorney, serve two main purposes.

The reason many novice inventors believe that they need NDA's is to obtain the acknowledgement of the recipient that the idea was shown to him in order to prevent idea theft. While it does serve as a psychological and possibly a legal deterrent for idea theft, the NDA also serves another, arguably even more important function. The United States Patent and Trademark Office (USPTO) has an inflexible rule regarding filing for patent protection. This rule states that an inventor has one year from the date of the first public disclosure of his invention in which to file for a patent. In other words, if you disclose your invention idea to anyone other than a close family member it could be considered a public disclosure. This would start the clock ticking and make it imperative for you to file for your patent within a year from that disclosure. The way to avoid this and give yourself additional time before you are required to file your patent application is to always use non-disclosure agreements when you discuss your invention with others. Patent attorneys and patent agents are an exception to this public disclosure rule. It is not necessary to obtain their signatures on non-disclosure agreements since disclosing your invention to these intellectual property professionals is not considered a "public" disclosure.

 Remember, if you make a public disclosure of your invention more than a year before filing for your patent, you give up all rights to ever file for a patent on that invention.

Novice inventors are often apologetic about asking others to sign NDA's, fearing that it will make it seem that they don't trust the recipients. It is understandable that they might feel this way, but anyone whose intentions are pure will be happy to sign the non-disclosure. If you are hesitant to ask someone to sign an NDA, simply tell them that you are doing it to protect your patent application filing date. It's the truth.

While someone with an ulterior motive could conceivably sign the agreement and then steal the idea, the NDA will prove that the idea was shown to him on a specific date. Also, although inventors do need to be protective of their ideas, there are not a lot of idea thieves around simply because inventing is neither the easiest nor the fastest way to make money. It has been our experience that most people who would steal are not willing to do all that is necessary to bring an idea to fruition. Additionally, creative people have their own ideas and would generally prefer to develop those than to steal an idea from someone else.

Now you know the two main reasons for NDA's. What do you do with them after they are signed by the recipient and who gets a copy? NDA's are only needed by the inventor, the owner of the invention idea. Once you have the document signed by the person to whom you will disclose your invention, you will place it into your files as proof of when and to whom you disclosed the invention. The person who signs your NDA has no need for a copy. If he insists on having a copy, which isn't likely, it's okay to give him one, but the document is intended for the inventor, not the recipient.

Occasionally a professional to whom you show your idea may request a copy of the NDA he signs for you. This is simply for his records so that he will know exactly what he has been shown, when, and by whom. There is no harm in providing one for him or in allowing him to make a copy.

Types of Non-Disclosure Agreements

There are two basic types of non-disclosure agreements that are important to the independent inventor; the Standard and the Contractor non-disclosure agreements. The standard agreement is the one that you will use when you share your invention idea with friends, colleagues, etc. This is the agreement that you will use most often.

The Contractor non-disclosure agreement is for your use when you are enlisting the assistance of someone with the actual development of the invention. Usually this is someone who is working with your prototype, but it could be anyone who is involved with any changes or additions that might be made to the invention. In the contractor non-disclosure agreement, the recipient acknowledges that he is being hired to do a job for you and that, if in fulfilling that duty, he makes suggestions or changes that become a part of the invention, those changes belong to you, the inventor. He acknowledges that any changes or additions he contributes do not make him a co-inventor of the item.

Where do you obtain blank NDA's? Blank non-disclosure agreements are widely available at no cost. You will find them in inventor help books, such as this one and on trusted inventor websites. We include one of each type of NDA on the next several pages, and samples of both types of NDA's are on our website that you may print and use as you wish. You will find these forms at:

`asktheinventors.com/nondisclosure.htm`

While NDA's are pretty standard in their wording, you might want to have your own attorney to look over any form that you intend to use to make sure that it will give you the protection that you need.

USPTO Disclosure Document Program

We have discussed Non-Disclosure Agreements. Now, we will explain the USPTO's Disclosure Document program. This is another important part of your "paper trail" of proof of when you started work on your invention. The Disclosure Document is a document that you will actually file with the patent office and receive a dated receipt from them. You can do this yourself, without the help of an attorney, and it costs only $10.00 to file. There are those who argue that this document is not necessary and perhaps it is not. But, as an independent inventor, you may be called upon to prove when you began working on your invention.

The Disclosure Document is something that actually remains on file at the USPTO for 2 years and it is something for which you will have a receipt from the patent office. Pretty powerful proof if you need it and it costs only $10.00 to file. The USPTO is considering discontinuing the Disclosure Document Program. So long as it is available we recommend that independent inventors take advantage of this inexpensive method of documenting the inception of their invention ideas.

The Disclosure Document is exactly that, a disclosure of your invention idea to the patent office. It is not a patent application and they will keep it for only two years. But, you will have your receipt from them for your files in case you should ever need it.

Find out everything you need to know about the USPTO's Disclosure Document Program at:

www.uspto.gov/web/offices/pac/disdo.html

Then, if you like, you can print out the cover page to use at:

www.uspto.gov/web/forms/sb0095.pdf

This cover page is a PDF document so you will need to have Adobe® Acrobat Reader installed on your computer in order to access this one. Adobe® Acrobat Reader is a free download and you can get it at:

www.download-it-free.com/acrobat

If you will purchase an inexpensive composition book for less than three dollars, make liberal use of non-disclosure agreements (both types), and file your Disclosure Document with the USPTO for only $10.00, you will have gone a long way toward protecting your invention. These are early-stage protective measures that are easy and inexpensive, but they can be very important if you should ever need to provide legal proof of when you began working on your invention.

Standard Non-Disclosure Agreement example:

CONFIDENTIAL DISCLOSURE AGREEMENT

This Agreement is between

_____,

hereinafter called "Recipient", and

_____,

hereinafter called "Owner".

WHEREAS Owner possesses certain confidential information concerning:

_____

_____

and

(Describe subject matter of information)

WHEREAS Recipient is desirous of obtaining said confidential information for purposes of evaluation
thereof and as a basis for further discussions with
Owner regarding assistance with development of the
confidential information for the benefit of Owner or
for the mutual benefit of Owner and Recipient;

THEREFORE, Recipient hereby agrees to receive the information in confidence and to treat it as confidential
for all purposes. Recipient will not divulge or use
in any manner any of said confidential information unless by written consent from Owner, and Recipient
wilL use at least the same efforts it regularly em-
ploys for its own confidential information to avoid
disclosure to others.

(SEE NEXT PAGE)

Standard Non-Disclosure Agreement:(continued)

CONFIDENTIAL DISCLOSURE AGREEMENT (continued)

PROVIDED, however, that this obligation to treat information confidentially will not apply to any information already in Recipient's possession or to any information that is generally available to the public or becomes generally available through no act or influence of Recipient. Recipient will inform Owner of the public nature or Recipient's possession of the information without delay after Owner's disclosure thereof or will be stopped from asserting such as defense to remedy under this agreement.

Recipient will exercise its best efforts to conduct its evaluation within a reasonable time after Owner's disclosure and will provide Owner with its assessment thereof without delay. Recipient will return all information, including all copies thereof, to Owner upon request. This agreement shall remain in effect for ten years after the date of its execution, and it shall be construed under the laws of the State of Texas.

_____/_____
(Recipient)   (Date)

By:_____/_____
    (Name & title of person signing)

_____/_____
(Owner)   (Date)

Contractor's Non-Disclosure Agreement example:

CONFIDENTIALITY AND SAFEGUARD AGREEMENT

This agreement is between

_____,

whose place of residence or business is

_____,

hereafter known as the inventor, and

_____,

whose place of business or residence is

_____,

hereafter known as the vendor.

Vendor will provide certain services as follows:

[ ]   prototyping

[ ]   design and/or drafting

[ ]   marketability evaluation and/or research
      and/or plan

[ ]   overall planning for development, protection,
      and marketing.

[ ]   other: _____

Vendor agrees to maintain all information divulged
to him or her by inventor, in whatever form (written,
drawn, photographed, verbal, video, or other), confidential and safe. Vendor will not transmit or divulge
said information to any third person (except his or
her employee who has a need to know). Vendor will
not use said information as his or her own, or for
his or her own advantage.

(SEE NEXT PAGE)

Contractor's Non-Disclosure Agreement (continued):

CONFIDENTIALITY AND SAFEGUARD AGREEMENT(continued)

Vendor will preserve as confidential and safe, said information for a period of _____ from date of order, and will:

[ ] return to inventor, or

[ ] destroy tangibles by shredding or burning after said period.

Vendor further agrees that all patentable features arising from his or her services will be revealed to the inventor as the work progresses, and become inventor's property in full at the time the vendor receives payment in amount agreed to by vendor and inventor at the time inventor's order is placed. Vendor further agrees that he/she has no claim to any intellectual property rights related to this invention.

_____/_____
(Vendor)   (Date)

CHAPTER SIX

Make A Prototype.

Prototyping is fun!

In our opinion, prototyping your invention is the fun part of inventing. For most of us, when that light bulb moment first occurs, we cannot wait to create a working model and try out our idea. After all, the reason we came up with the idea in the first place was to solve a problem, right? And we are eager to prove that our idea will solve that problem. Or that it will be a better way to accomplish some task that we do on a regular basis. Here, we will discuss some prototyping options for the Shoestring Budget™ inventor.

While some of our ideas to improve the world are far too technical or complicated for us even to create a prototype, many of the best inventions are simple improvements on existing products. We have already suggested in an earlier chapter that Shoestring Budget™ inventors should stick to their simpler ideas for their first ventures into product development. This is because it is much easier to accomplish with a simple invention. But, it is also because simpler inventions generally cost far less for many of the steps in the process. Certainly, a prototype that you can create or have made inexpensively will help you to stay within your shoestring budget.

What if your great idea is something that is so technical or complicated that it requires the assistance of experts? You may still be able to accomplish it but you may have to come up with some additional funding.

Why bother with a prototype?

Your prototype (working model of your invention) serves several functions:

- First, it proves what your idea is and that it actually works as you believe it will work.

- Second, it serves as a sample of the eventual product for use in getting the product made if you plan to be the manufacturer, or to demonstrate your invention to a potential licensee when you show it for licensing.

- It is your opportunity to fine tune the invention and make improvements. It also helps you to think up every possible use for your invention. This is important to your eventual patent application.

- It can also be used for focus groups and surveys to determine the marketability of the product. And, the very act of creating the prototype serves an educational function for the inventor.

Very Simple Ideas

If your idea is something for which you can make your first crude prototype from something that you have around the house or in your garage, chances are that you have already done this. The excitement of a new idea propels us to try anything that we have at hand to see if it will work. A prototype is simply a working model, to prove an invention. Often, the first prototype of a new invention bears little or no resemblance to the final product. That's okay.

Remember that a prototype has to prove only three things: what the idea is, how it works, and that it does work. Initial prototypes should be as inexpensive as you can possibly make them.

When that great idea first occurred to you, you probably visualized it in its final form and you knew exactly what it would be made from and what it would look like. Or, so you thought. One of the most important jobs an inventor has is to create the prototype. And, one of the first lessons the new inventor learns is that, no matter how simple the idea, he is likely to go through quite a number of prototypes before settling on the final version.

One comment that we frequently hear from new inventors is, "Oh, I don't need to make a prototype. I know it will work!" Especially when an invention is so simple that it doesn't take a rocket scientist to create it. Here is a story that illustrates why this kind of thinking this is a big mistake.

When we first began working on our **Ghostline®** product, we didn't think prototyping would be any big deal. Our invention involved lines on paper. How hard can that be? We would begin by preparing a poster board the same way we had always done it, by measuring with a yardstick and drawing light pencil lines on the board. Then, we would just have a printer to do the same thing we had done using ink. Sounds easy, right? That's what we thought.

The first thing we learned is that there were no available inks that could print ghosted lines such as could be made using a pencil. An ink formulation would have to be developed to achieve that effect. Our goal was to have lines that would be clearly visible for the person who was making the poster and then for the lines to virtually disappear after the poster was completed. With that in mind, and possessing creative natures, we began exploring what colors other than light gray might work even better for this purpose. We tried light blue, thinking it might work since it is used for copying documents without having the lines to show. We could see the lines from across the room! Then, we tried light yellow lines. We thought we had the solution with yellow because those lines were visible enough for the user to see in order to create the poster but they were almost invisible once the poster was created. This seemed perfect, so we had a batch printed using yellow lines. Under the fluorescent lights of a retail store or the printers shop, those yellow lines were great. Then, we took the poster board home and under the incandescent lights used in homes, the lines vanished! They just disappeared. What a shock that was! It was something that we could not have anticipated. Only with experimentation did we come to realize that the type of lighting where the boards were used would play a part in how visible the lines would be.

We were back to the drawing board. We didn't want the lines to disappear *before* the poster board was used. Several experiments later, we came up with the exact right ink formulation; a concoction of black, white, and silver, that became the final product. This is the nature of prototyping.

The point here is that we could not have anticipated those problems. We had to actually make the poster boards in the various colors and test them to see what worked. When you are working with your prototype, you will think of improvements that had not occurred to you and you are likely to encounter problems that also had not occurred to you. This is a vital part of the process because if you have a wonderful, successful product, you can be sure that others will want to share your success. If you do not take the time and effort to build every possible improvement into your invention, the next person could come along and make those improvements, making your invention obsolete.

The education that comes with it is another benefit gained from creating your own prototype. You will learn more than you ever thought you would by becoming intimately acquainted with how your product will be made. This will stand you in good stead later. If you become your own manufacturer, you will certainly need to know everything there is to know about the product. If you plan to license the invention, you will need a good understanding of what goes into making the product in order to work out your best deal. Your potential licensee will expect you to know more about your product than he does in the beginning.

Remember that your prototype can be made from anything at all that will allow you to see that it works. Even if your invention would eventually be made from metal or plastic, if you can make a cardboard model that proves the viability of the idea, that is fine for the first prototype.

Where to Find Parts for Your Prototype

If you need parts for your prototype and you don't know where to find them, think of what objects already contain those parts. For example, if you need parts that are already found in a clock, a cassette tape player, a toy with moving parts, etc., perhaps you can obtain one of those items at a garage sale or purchase an inexpensive model at a discount store. Taking apart an inexpensive item in order to use its parts is often far less expensive than buying those parts separately, if you are even able to find the exact parts to purchase.

Some very good aids are now available for novice inventors who want to make good-looking plastic prototypes. If you want to make your own plastic prototypes from materials that are readily available, Randall Landreneau, a Florida inventor and former president of the Tampa Bay Inventors Council, has both a book and a video teaching you how to do that. Randall understands that the independent inventor needs a prototype that will show off his invention to its best advantage and one that does not require a large investment to create. The method he has developed allows you to do exactly that. You can find out about this method on his website:

www.plasticprototypes.net

A discount coupon for Randall Landreneau's video, "Make Your Own Plastic Prototypes," can be found in the back of this book.

If you want a good-looking plastic prototype (even if your eventual product will be made of metal), but you don't want to make it yourself, there is now an inexpensive way to get that done. Just a few years ago, the only way to get a plastic prototype was by use of an injection mold. Injection molds are necessary for most final products that are made from plastic or metal, and they can cost thousands or even hundreds of thousands of dollars. But, they are not necessary during the early prototyping stage. Even if you could afford to have a special injection mold made for your invention, it would be foolhardy to do it early in your prototyping process or before you have the final version of the product and a solid marketing plan in place. For this reason, until the early 1990's independent inventors were handicapped if their inventions required an injection mold. But now, thanks to a process known as rapid prototyping, a great-looking plastic prototype is within the reach of the Shoestring Budget™ inventor. These prototypes, made by several different methods, but all involving the use of 3-D stereolithography, are now widely available. Many individual prototype designers now have the equipment to create these prototypes and the price is based on the amount of raw plastic material used. It is a good idea to check prices in your area but it may be possible to get your prototype made for as little as $48.00 per cubic inch of material used.

While prototypes made by this method are usually excellent for demonstration purposes, they are not durable and could not be used as a finished product would be used. But, they are beautiful and they have the look of a shelf-ready product. To find someone in your area who can create these plastic prototypes, look in your Internet search engine for Rapid Prototyping. You will find contact information on the "Resources" page in the back of this book for one such company. There is also a coupon in our coupon pages for a discount on this type of prototype.

If your prototype does not lend itself to one of the previously mentioned methods and you feel that you cannot, or don't wish to make your prototype, there are places to get that accomplished. Here is another area for you to put your creativity into play. While there are people whose business it is to create prototypes, you may be able to get your prototype made by someone who is not specifically identified as a prototype designer, but who can do exactly what you want; an artisan or craftsman who works with the materials you wish to use. For example, your prototype maker could be someone in a metal or woodworking shop, a tailor, a printer, etc. It can be anyone who has the capability of building your prototype.

Avoid disclosing your invention to someone who will create your prototype without first getting a signed non-disclosure agreement. Remember, this is considered a public disclosure if you do not get the document signed for your files.

We know of some inventors who were using vinyl file folders as the material to create prototypes of their idea. They were unable to find any adhesive that would bond the vinyl to itself. It simply popped apart after the adhesives dried. Thinking creatively, they took the folders to a tailor and, after getting a signed contractor's non-disclosure agreement, told him where they wanted the pieces joined. The tailor sewed the prototypes and they worked just fine to prove what the invention idea was and how it worked. The final product could easily be heat bonded and the manufacturer knew this, so sewing the prototypes together was a good, inexpensive solution to the bonding problem.

Professional Prototype Designers

Perhaps your idea is so new and innovative that you need the help of a prototype designer to create it. You should be able to find these people listed in your telephone directory under "Prototypes". Or, check with your nearest inventor organization or club. There are many such clubs scattered across the country and you will find a list of them in Appendix A in the back of this book. The members of these clubs are familiar with the local resources and sometimes these organizations even have prototype designers among the membership. Professional prototype designers should have a contractor's non-disclosure agreement that they will sign for you, but just in case, take your own form and get it signed before disclosing the idea to them.

In order to avoid misunderstandings regarding exactly how your prototype is to look and function, it is sometimes helpful to have some really good graphics to provide to your prototype designer. If you are unable to do these precise types of computer drawings, there are artisans who can do it for you. One such graphic artist whose work and reputation we know is Fred Fleming [**fredfleming.com**]. Fred is located in North Carolina but he works with inventors across the country. The fees Fred charges for his clear and precise artwork are among the lowest we have found.

 Fred Fleming offers a variety of graphic art services to help inventors develop and promote their concepts. A discount coupon for these services can be found in the back of this book.

Prototypes for Licensing

If you plan to license your invention for royalties, you will want to take a prototype with you when you meet with the manufacturer. Does an acceptable prototype have to be expensive? Not at all. In most cases, it can be very inexpensive indeed. Your prototype needs only to show what the invention is, how it works and that it does work. Manufacturers that have in-house product development divisions make prototypes from whatever materials are available, just as you do. They realize that your prototype is just that . . . a working model. They do not expect a finished product that looks at this point as if it could be on the retail store shelf.

Having said that, let us emphasize that your prototype should look as good as you can make it look. It might not be made from the materials that the final product would be made. This is not important at this stage. But, if you can make it look as good as possible, it will help the manufacturer to visualize it as a part of his product line.

By now, you can see that it is possible to make decent looking prototypes from materials that are readily available to you and keep the prototyping costs down. And attractive packaging can be created for very little expense if you utilize the information you can get from manufacturer's websites. With a little ingenuity and some inexpensive clear labels from the office supply store, you can place the logo of your target manufacturing company right on your prototype. In this way, you will have the exact font and color of that company's packaging. Simply copy and paste the logo into your word processing program and print it onto clear labels. These labels can then be attached to the prototype itself or to whatever packaging you design for the prototype.

Make it look like it belongs in the manufacturer's product line

The idea is to make your prototype look like a product from that manufacturer's product line. It is an amazing fact that some product development people at these large companies simply do not grasp the concept of new products that they should easily grasp, especially when the new products fit right into their present lines. So, your task is to do their thinking for them. Don't leave anything to chance. Put anything that you want to be sure they "get" clearly on the prototype itself or into your written presentation, or both.

CHAPTER SEVEN

Ask The Experts.

Why have a product evaluation?

As a Shoestring Budget™ inventor, you may be tempted to skip having a professional marketability study performed on your invention. This is a sore temptation for most independent inventors. After all, you know that your product will succeed in the marketplace, right? Could it be that your total faith in your product idea has blinded you to basic market considerations that could affect whether or not your product will succeed? If so, you would not be the first. We cannot count the number of people who have written to us at Ask the Inventors! who have been adamant that they did not need a professional product evaluation. We once had an inventor who told us that he had invented something that almost everyone in the world would want and need. (That was a dead give away that this 'inventor' was in La La Land! If there is an invention that is needed by everyone in the world we haven't seen it.) He had invented an umbrella to provide shade for trees! We explained that we were confused. Weren't trees a virtual umbrella themselves providing shade and protection? "Oh, no," he explained, "Sometimes it is too hot for trees to grow well." Setting aside the practical aspects of his invention idea, he had not even considered how such a tree umbrella could be put up or taken down. He clearly had not thought his idea through. He was so sure that his idea was a great one that he refused to even consider that he might need a professional evaluation. Often, the inventors who are most adamant that they do not need a professional evaluation are the ones who need it the most.

Some inventors may have a good idea but they are not experienced with the retail market and have no idea if the product can be produced cheaply enough to make it a profitable product. Or, they do not know what the competition for that particular product is or how much market resistance there might be to their product. By market resistance, we mean that sometimes a product that appears to be viable fails to catch buyer interest for reasons that are not always immediately apparent. When this happens to the independent inventor due to his failure to carefully investigate the market for the product, it is a sad, expensive lesson.

A professional marketability evaluation is essential for most every independent inventor. This is one of those times when you will need to spend a little money. It may well save you a great deal of money in the long run if the marketability study prevents you from rushing to market with a product that is not ready to be marketed in its present form or is destined to fail.

Cost of a professional product evaluation

Professional marketability evaluations can be obtained for a range of prices. We would encourage even a Shoestring Budget™ inventor to get the best marketability evaluation he can afford. The price range varies from around $300 to $600. Obviously, the evaluations in the lower price range provide less information than the more expensive ones. The less expensive legitimate evaluations that we are aware of are available through the I2 **Innovation Institute** at:

www.wini2.com

and the **United Inventors' Association's Innovation Assessment Program** at:

www.uiausa.com/Services/IAP/UIAIAP.htm

Both services consist of an evaluation based on a formula weighing specific market factors and conditions.

Even though neither evaluation is the most thorough one available, they both are certainly worthwhile. The evaluations they provide can point out the strengths and weaknesses of your product and give direction on how best to improve on its weak areas in order to maximize your chances of success before entering the market.

The more thorough product evaluation services such as the one offered by the **University of Wisconsin Innovation Service Center** at:

www.academics.uww.edubusiness/innovate/contact_us.htm

are more expensive (around $600) but you receive much more for the investment. Hiring one of the thorough product evaluation services is like hiring a team of consultants. They will analyze your competition, the market resistance to your product, how much consumer education will be required for your product to be embraced by the public, probable cost to manufacture your product and an overall assessment of your product's probable success or failure in the marketplace. In some cases, they will even identify likely licensing partners.

 The University of Wisconsin hosts an annual Ideas to Profits seminar. There is a coupon for 20% off admission to this great event in the coupon section at the back of this book.

The University of Wisconsin's Innovation Service Center is not the only such service available. There are others scattered around the country. A university near you may offer a similar service. Call the business or entrepreneurial department of nearby universities to see if they offer professional product evaluation services. Small Business Development Centers that are usually affiliated with community colleges may also be a source of legitimate product evaluation services. Call your local SBDC to see if they offer such a service in your community.

Still another source for a limited product evaluation service is through legitimate licensing agents. Their evaluation, however, is not an overall product evaluation; it is merely an evaluation of whether their company would be interested in representing your product for licensing. Most of these companies, like **Harvey Reese and Associates** at:

www.money4ideas.com

charge a fee of around $200 to evaluate whether or not your product is one they would like to represent. If they do select your product and they are able to obtain a license agreement for you then they would share in your royalties, usually between 30% and 60%. You can find other legitimate licensing agents from reliable sources such as **Inventors Digest Magazine** at:

www.inventorsdigest.com

or **The United Inventors' Association** at:

www.uiausa.org

or from our website, **Ask the Inventors!** at:

www.asktheinventors.com

Scam Companies

For Shoestring Budget™ inventors it is as important to know whom you should not hire to perform your product evaluation as it is to know whom you should hire. Many Shoestring Budget™ inventors have lost thousands of their hard-earned dollars because they fell victim to the slick ads of companies that are only interested in getting their money, not in evaluating, patenting or obtaining licenses for their clients. How can you know who those companies are? How do you know if you are dealing with a trustworthy company? There are a few telltale signs that you are dealing with a scam company. First and foremost, use extreme caution regarding any company that advertises on television or radio. You may also see print ads for them in trusted print publications. Or, they are listed first or have paid advertising on the major search engines. The legitimate product evaluation services do not normally use expensive advertising because they have more business than they can handle from word-of-mouth referrals and they do not need to advertise other than in **Inventors' Digest Magazine** or on the **United Inventors' Association** website.

You may be saying to yourself, "But, what about the companies I see advertised on trusted stations like CNN or Discovery? Or, what about the advertisement I saw in Popular Mechanics Magazine or Discovery Magazine?" Our advice stands; be wary about trusting any company you see or hear advertised in any of the high dollar advertising venues! Those networks, magazines and search engines are in the business of selling advertising, not in checking their legitimacy.

Another telltale sign that you are probably dealing with a scam company is that they offer to send you a "free inventor's kit." If you sign up with one of those companies, you are likely to pay very dearly for that "free" kit in the long run.

 The materials in the "free" inventor's kits that are offered by the questionable invention promotion companies are also free from the USPTO's website...with no strings attached!

Finally, after you have contacted one of these companies they will pursue you relentlessly. They will tell you what a fantastic product idea you have and they will tell you that you are going to make millions as they pressure you with phone calls and letters to sign on with them before a deadline. Legitimate companies would never pressure you in this way. Beware! The scam companies, on the other hand, tell almost every person they speak to that his product is destined to be a huge hit in the marketplace and they attempt to sign up 95%+ of the people who contact them. The legitimate companies turn down 95% of the people who contact them. If your product is one of the 5% selected for marketing by one of the legitimate marketing companies, you can be sure that it will have at least a chance of ending up on store shelves.

Victim of a scam company? What you can do.

If you have found yourself in the position of being one of the thousands and thousands of victims of these scam companies you can take heart that many, many other very intelligent people have also fallen for their slick sales pitches. Their promises to do everything from evaluating to patenting and marketing sound extremely attractive to those of us who are busy with our jobs and day-to-day life and who fear that we do not have the time or expertise to pursue our great idea. They promise to handle it all for us. For those of us who are accustomed to delegating tasks to employees and colleagues, it seems like a natural thing to do.

If you have had an unfortunate encounter with one of these companies, it is unlikely that you will ever recover any of your money. You should however, report them to the **Federal Trade Commission** and the **USPTO**. The FTC and the USPTO both maintain lists of invention promotion companies that have had complaints lodged against them. Both of these U. S. government offices make the lists available for public viewing. You may not get your money back but you may be able to forewarn another prospective victim. You may file a complaint with the **Federal Trade Commission** at:

https://rn.ftc.gov/pls/dod/wsolcq$.startup?Z_ORG_CODE=PU01

or with the **United States Patent and Trademark Office** at:

www.uspto.gov/web/forms/2048.pdf

It is also a good idea to report them to **R.J. Riley's** website,

www.inventored.org

He maintains both a "caution" and an "extreme caution" list of invention promotion companies that have had consumer complaints filed or reported against them.

Pricing Your Product

Although this section is not necessarily about how to save money during the inventive process, we are including it because it involves money and it is a way independent inventors inadvertently sabotage themselves. Too often, an independent inventor has an unrealistic expectation of what his invention will sell for in the retail market. This usually happens for a couple of reasons. First, he thinks his invention is just fabulous and he speculates that if such an item were available he would be willing to pay "X" number of dollars for it.

We once had an inventor who came to us with a rubber glove tip to be used on the thumb when playing a video game. The tip could be manufactured for a fraction of a penny, but he thought he could sell them for ten or fifteen dollars each! He thought they were just the greatest thing ever and he assumed everyone who played video games would want them. This inventor reasoned that since video games sell for $50 or more for each game, the gamers should be willing to pay $10-$15 for his thumb tip that he believed would give them more control.

This man had, in effect, pulled his retail-selling price out of thin air. That is a common mistake made by novice inventors. When he presented his idea to prospective licensees and told them what he thought the retail selling price should be, the manufacturers immediately dismissed him as being totally unrealistic. The remainder of his product presentation was also dismissed because he was then seen as a flake, definitely not someone with whom they would want to negotiate a license agreement since he had already come across to them as someone with completely unreasonable expectations.

The second way independent product developers come up with retail pricing that is simply not feasible is by taking their pricing cues from friends and family, who are well-meaning but not helpful in this regard.

When we were first developing our **Ghostline®** poster board product and we asked the people closest to us what they would be willing to pay we heard totally unrealistic prices. Our mom said she thought it was so great and it would save so much time and effort (echoing what we had told her) that she would be willing to pay $2.99 per sheet! We loved hearing that but even we realized that no one in their right mind would pay $2.99 for a sheet of poster board, even if it did have faint lines. Our mom loves us. She was sincere, but without meaning to, she was telling us what she thought we wanted to hear; not what she would have been willing to pay for a poster board with a faint grid -- not invented by us -- if she had found it in the store on her own.

Other relatives and friends also told us inflated prices they would be willing to pay for **Ghostline®** if it were available in the stores. Again, they were telling us what they thought we wanted to hear. It wasn't until we were actually manufacturing and selling it ourselves that we realized that $1 per sheet is about the maximum anyone will pay for a poster board with a ghosted grid. Luckily for us, however, that price allowed for a nice profit for everyone involved in its selling.

Without realizing it, we had managed to stay within the pricing guidelines for a successful retail item. We later learned that the rule of thumb in pricing your product is that its retailselling price should be approximately four to five times the manufacturing cost. The manufacturing cost of some items, such as our **Ghostline®**, is actually a tenth or less of the retail selling price (even better!), but that is not the norm.

When you purchase a retail product for $10 you can assume that it cost around $2 - $2.50 to manufacture. It was then sold to the retailer for a wholesale price of around $5 and then to you, the consumer, for $10. This is the way it works 90% of the time. You can readily see that this pricing structure allows for a nice margin of profit for all the parties involved in moving a product from manufacture to the store shelves.

If your invention will cost $10 to manufacture, this means your product should be priced at no more than $40-$50 in the marketplace. If it is unrealistic to believe your product can sell for that amount, then you should seriously consider abandoning this invention idea for your next great idea.

If your product will not fit within this formula, it is unlikely that you will be able to find a manufacturer who is willing to license it. That is just the hard economic truth of one of the major concerns and decision making factors manufacturers take into account when determining whether they should license a particular product.

Remember the woman we spoke about in Chapter 2 who had invented the new type of glasses lenses? She is the perfect example of someone who had a great product and a great idea but she had not done her homework to see if the product would be economically feasible in the marketplace. Making sure that your product will fit comfortably into this formula will help you to be realistic in the proposed pricing of your product. That, in turn, will help you to be taken more seriously by possible licensing partners and make it easier for the manufacturers to see that your product will make money for them.

Offshore Manufacturing

When you are determining the manufacturing cost for your product, one cost saving option is to have it costed by offshore manufacturers as well as domestic manufacturers. Often the costs of having your product made in the Orient are a fraction of domestic manufacturing costs. When you are presenting your product for possible licensing it shows that you have done your homework and know what you are talking about if you can discuss the price spread between domestic and offshore manufacturing. Also, if offshore manufacturing is significantly lower than domestic manufacturing (and it usually is) your licensing partner will undoubtedly have it manufactured outside of this country.

How do you find someone to get your product costed offshore? You contact someone who has done it before. Your local inventors club will undoubtedly have members who have had their products made offshore. Ask them who they used and if they were satisfied with the service. You can also find them through legitimate organizations such as the **United Inventors' Association** at:

www.uiausa.org

or publications like **Inventors' Digest Magazine**.

If your product is a textile, Edith Tolchin of EGT Global Trading is a reliable and reasonable source of help with offshore pricing and manufacturing. You can reach her at:

www.hometown.aol.com/egtglobaltrading

She comes highly recommended by both the United Inventors' Association and Inventors' Digest Magazine.

If You Don't Know Your Manufacturing Costs

What if you simply are unable, for whatever reason, to find out the probable manufacturing cost of your product? There is a way to get a very general and imperfect "guesstimate" of what the cost might be by using the pricing formula we discussed earlier, but in reverse. Go to a store. Look for products that are made of similar materials in approximately the same basic amounts as your product. It does not have to be a similar product. It can be a completely different category of product so long as the materials of which it is made are in approximately the same proportions. Look at the retail cost and work backwards.

For example, if the retail product sells for $20, you can assume that the wholesale price was half of that amount, or $10. The manufacturing cost likely was half of that amount, or $5. You can assume from this that your product might be made for around $5. This is extremely inaccurate and only gives you an approximation of the probable manufacturing cost. This method, obviously, does not take into consideration the complexity of the product or steps required to make it and should only be used when there is no alternative. If you are unable to come up with a reasonable cost estimate for manufacturing your product, this may be strong motivation to get that professional evaluation. Having this important information provided may be worth the cost of the evaluation in itself.

You can see from this chapter that it is very important for the Shoestring Budget™ inventor to have as thorough a marketability study as possible and as accurate an estimate of manufacturing costs as possible in order to maximize his chances of success. It is a shame when a Shoestring Budget™ inventor has worked diligently to cut costs and save money throughout the process but does not get his product to market because of failure in these two crucial areas. In that case, even though he may not have spent a large sum on his invention, what he did spend was a waste. Don't let this happen to you.

CHAPTER EIGHT

Need Money?

Finding the Money

It is often the case that an individual who is very creative about coming up with a great idea does not use that same creativity when it comes to finding the money to move forward with it. It is our aim in this chapter to shed some light on how to approach the problem of funding your invention.

As a Shoestring Budget™ inventor, the very first place you should look for help is in your mirror. We know that is not what you want to hear, but it is the truth of the matter. Before others would even consider investing in your idea they would need to see that you had enough faith in your idea to put your own money where your mouth is. Many independent inventors have the very mistaken notion that the idea for a terrific new product is contribution enough on their part. Wrong!

Your Personal Savings

Shoestring Budget™ inventing does not mean cost-free inventing. If only that were the case! It means that you must contribute, at least some of your own money, to the project. You may be saying, "But, I don't have any money!" If that is the case, then you might as well stop now. Almost anyone can tap into savings or plan for future expenditures by saving small amounts as they can for something that is really important to them. As we mentioned in an earlier chapter, an inventing project does not require that you have the entire amount at the start. It is very possible to pay for your invention in segments as you move through the steps. In fact, that is the way it must be done since product development, protection and marketing take place over a somewhat extended period of time and the expenditures are made in different areas, such as prototyping, legal, and so on.

When we were first inventing our product, **Ghostline** ®, we were the epitome of Shoestring Budget™ inventors. We were a couple of wives and mothers who were working full time jobs and we did not have a lot of expendable income. We did have faith in our idea; enough faith to dip into our savings to get our first prototypes made. We did it in bits and pieces. First, we each contributed about $200, when that money was exhausted we each dipped into our savings again to replenish our "company fund" in order to have the money to continue the prototyping process. Thankfully, our first visits to patent attorneys were free (we interviewed several patent attorneys before selecting one) but when the time came to start the patent application we each dipped into our family savings again.

If you truly have faith in the potential of your idea, you will be willing to invest at least some of your own money. If you do not have enough faith in your idea to put your money, even if it is limited, where your mouth is, stop now. Do not waste your time or anyone else's.

Pay-As-You-Go

Expenses during the development, protection and marketing phases of inventing do not all occur at once. There is no need to have all the money that will be spent on the project at the beginning of the process. Very few independent inventors have a surplus amount of money set aside with which to pursue their product ideas. Most of us are operating on shoestring budgets. Many have succeeded and so can you. It may be necessary to save for a while and then move to the next phase of your product development. Then save again for the next phase and so on. As you read this book – or any book that details the steps in product development – you will see that there are lots of details related to your invention that you could be doing while you are saving between expenditures. So, it isn't as if you have to spend all of your time in a holding pattern while you accumulate the needed funds.

Personal Checking or Savings Accounts

If you can finance your invention from your own funds, this is the very best, least complicated way to go. We did exactly this with a twist. As we have previously mentioned, quite a lot of the initial steps were funded by our personal savings. Once we were patent pending we started manufacturing and selling **Ghostline®** on a limited basis. We loaded up the trunk of the car with 100-piece packages and drove around selling it to local independent teacher stores and office supply stores. We made enough money doing this to pay the legal fees when our First Office Action came back from the patent office. An Office Action is any correspondence that comes from the USPTO relating to your application for protection of your intellectual property, whether it is a patent application or a trademark application. Office Actions require a response from whomever is prosecuting your application.

We also made enough money from sales of the poster board to pay for the next run of the product. Several times we repeated the cycle of manufacturing small runs and then selling it to earn enough money for the next run and to pay patent related expenses until we finally received notice that our patent would be allowed. So, even though we weren't selling a lot of **Ghostline®**, we were "in the black." We were covering our expenses as we went.

By proceeding in the pay-as-you-go mode we kept complete control of our product and our company. For us, it was the right decision. Success might have come sooner had we gotten investors or loans, but the comfort of knowing that we were limiting our financial risk was worth the extra time it may have taken. Only you can decide if this is the proper course of action for you and your product. If your product is "time sensitive," that is if it is essential that you get to market as soon as possible or risk losing out entirely, you may need to consider the following options.

Hobby or Special Talent Income

If you have a special talent, hobby or skill that could create a little nest egg that could be allocated for your invention, this is a great way to come up with the needed cash. Do you have a service you can offer to make extra cash or a product that you can create and sell? Lots of people have taken the time to learn specialized crafting and they can make and sell products or offer a class to teach others the skill. We know of a man whose "regular" job is an airline pilot, but in his spare time, he designs and creates special t-shirts for charity events, sporting events, school groups and so on.

Think about what you like to do in your spare time. Do you play an instrument so that you could provide music for social occasions? Perhaps you know how to bake beautiful pastries or can sew like a professional. Can you groom pets or teach a craft? Get your creative juices flowing about what you could do in your spare time that would bring in the extra income to pay your invention costs.

Charge It!

If you do not have personal savings with which to fund your invention, you could use your credit cards. This is a slippery slope, however. Never charge more than you can easily pay back within a reasonably short time. Credit card interest rates are among the highest and using credit cards for large amounts that must be paid back over an extended period of time is not a wise course of action. It is appropriate to use your credit card for small purchases of prototype materials or prototyping services, for example, especially if you are like us and like to get air miles for nearly everything you purchase.

Loans

If you want to get others to help you with the expenses related to your product development, you have several options. First, you could go to your local bank or credit union and get a loan. Often you can get a signature loan, that is a loan without putting up any collateral, for $2,000 to $3,000 if you have a good record with the bank or institution (no bounced checks, etc.). That may be enough money to launch your quest.

If that amount is not enough to fund the initial phases of your invention (this would likely only be the case if your invention were technical or complicated), you could get a larger loan by putting up collateral. Most often people use their homes as collateral for larger loans. This is a perilous proposition and not one we would recommend. We know that you believe that your invention is a sure thing and we hope that it is, but there are so many variables involved with inventing that no invention, no matter how good, is a sure thing. If you do not have a way to pay back such a loan without counting on potential income earned from your invention, don't do it! No invention is worth risking your family's financial security. We once heard from a want-to-be inventor who had done that very thing. He had mortgaged his home and had no way to make the payments when his invention failed to produce the income he expected. He was evicted from his home and found himself and his family homeless! Don't let this happen to you!

The **Small Business Administration** is yet another possibility for obtaining a loan. SBA loans are actually loans you get through your local bank or credit union but they are guaranteed by the Small Business Administration. SBA loans are usually for between $10,000 and $150,000. They are most often given to small companies with a proven track record. They are seldom, if ever, given for something as speculative as an invention.

Your best chance of obtaining an SBA loan will be if you have established a business around your invention or you already have a small business and are simply incorporating your invention into your business.

Shares in your company

Another option for raising funds is to sell shares in the company you have created around your product. Often investors are more comfortable knowing that in return for their financial outlay they are getting actual ownership in your company in the form of shares. For example, you can issue 100 shares to represent the total value of your company and assign a monetary value to each share. If you choose to sell shares in your company, proceed with caution. You could end up with so many partners that it will be difficult to reach any consensus on even day-to-day business decisions. Or, in an effort to raise more money you could end up being a minority owner in your own company!

Insurance Policies

Your life insurance policy may have a cash value against which you can borrow. The interest rate for borrowing your own money, in effect, is usually lower than almost anywhere else you could borrow the money. If yours is a whole life policy, this may be a possible source of money that you could use in the development of your product. If it is a term policy, there will be no cash value option. Check with your insurance agent to see if this is a possibility for you. Be certain that borrowing against the cash value will not reduce the benefits to your family should something happen to you. No matter how great your invention and how much faith you have that it will be a fabulous financial success, the financial security of your family should be your first priority, not funding your invention. You can find creative ways to plan for expenses or obtain funds for your invention without putting your family at financial risk.

Investors

Almost every inventor who is operating on limited funds has had that "Aha" moment when they think, "I'll just tell someone my idea and they will see how terrific it is and want to give me money to develop it." If you are lucky enough to find someone who shares your enthusiasm for your product to the degree that he wants to invest his money in it, you should negotiate your arrangement with him in a professional manner. You will need to have a written contract that clearly delineates what he is giving you and what he is getting in return. Is he sharing in gross profits or net profits? How do you determine what those are to everyone's satisfaction? Will he have part ownership in your business or company? If so, how much? How much is too much? Will he have a percentage of your company or shares of company stock? How do you determine what is a fair percentage to give him in exchange for his financial investment? How much input will he have in the decision-making process of your company? Are you required to pay back his investment in addition to sharing profits? Does he understand the risks involved; that he may earn money on his investment or he may lose all of it? What happens in that case? Are you required to pay him back if that should happen?

If you are getting an investor it is a good idea to get a legal contract drawn up by an attorney to reduce the likelihood of misunderstandings down the line. This is true whether your investor is family, a friend, or merely a business acquaintance.

Where Can You Find Investors?

The first place to look for investors is among your family and friends. They love you. They want you to succeed and if you can convince them that you have a great invention idea, they may be willing to invest their money. For them, they are investing in you as well as your invention. They will undoubtedly be the easiest people in your circle of influence to convince to invest.

Second, look to acquaintances. This may be your doctor, lawyer, dentist, accountant, co-workers, etc. Professionals you know may be willing to invest some of their expendable income in your company/invention if you present your case in a compelling and convincing manner. The stock market has disillusioned many an investor in the last several years and these professionals may be willing to invest a small portion of their portfolio on your invention.

You will need to do your homework before you approach them. Don't just go in with a great idea. Before they are likely to invest their money they will want to see, at the very minimum, a business plan for developing and marketing your product. If you have not written a business plan, they are likely to see your project as entirely too risky.

You may be thinking, "I'll just go to a Venture Capitalist. Isn't that what they do?" The answer is no, rarely, if ever, for you as a small independent inventor. Venture Capitalists are the big time. They invest big money, to be sure, but they want a virtual guarantee that they are likely to make big money on their investment in a relatively short period of time. Independent inventing is entirely too risky for most Venture Capitalists. They are not an option for most independent inventors.

Investment angels, on the other hand, may be a possibility. Investment angels can be found informally among the people previously suggested: doctors, lawyers, accountants and so on. Or, they may be found in formal organizations. For example, many communities have investment angel groups. You can find listings for such groups in your local business journals. You can find links for several angel investment lists in Appendix B at the back of this book. You can also find angel investors by running a classified ad for them. Your ad should say something like, "Inventor seeks angel investor for patent-pending product. Small investment opportunity. (Your phone number)."

Classified newspaper or Internet ads that you find listing investment angels may or may not be legitimate! They are often "services" that promise to put you in touch with angel investors in exchange for a fee. It is best to find your own angel investors.

Professional Partners

Professional partners are a special category of partners. They do not invest money. Instead, they invest their professional services in exchange for a share of your invention or your business. Patent attorneys, patent agents, professional prototypers, accountants and contract attorneys all have the potential to be a professional partner. Before you get too excited that this will be a way that you can dramatically decrease your expenditures, be forewarned that professional partnerships are hard to come by. Some independent inventors think that when their patent attorney sees their great idea, he will eagerly barter his services for a share of the invention. This is rarely the case. Keep in mind; patent attorneys earn their living by seeing inventions every day, all day. They couldn't make a living if they traded their services for a share of each invention that came across their desks. We have heard of cases where a patent attorney did become a professional partner to an inventor but these cases are extremely rare. We mention it here only because it does happen on rare occasions and it may be worth it to you to suggest it if the individual you are working with indicates a strong enthusiasm for the invention. It is something that every patent attorney or patent agent has had suggested to him at one time or another. It doesn't hurt to ask. and he will not be offended if you ask, but don't get your hopes up.

Another potential professional partner is your prototype designer. Again, like the patent attorney and patent agent, this is something that is suggested to prototype designers with some regularity. Unless your invention is that one-in-a-million idea, your prototyper would probably prefer to be paid in money than to bet on the success of your invention.

Almost any professional whose services you will use in the development and marketing of your invention has the possibility of becoming a professional partner. If you choose to pursue this avenue, be cautious not to sign on too many professional partners. This is another area where you could find yourself in the position of becoming a minority investor/owner of your own invention.

Grants

Business communities across the country are beginning to recognize the value of independent inventors and offering research and development (R & D) money to inventors in a variety of ways. The Amarillo, Texas, inventor club has partnered with the Small Business Development Center and community leaders to establish a fund from which they award grants to deserving independent inventors. The State of Oregon also recently offered grants to deserving independent product developers. There are similar programs in other parts of the country. The availability and requirements for each of these programs varies from community to community. Contact your local inventor club or Small Business Development Center to see if such a program exists for inventors in your area.

Private Grants

In addition to grants offered by inventor clubs or the Small Business Development Centers, there may be other grants for which you would qualify. The main libraries in each community have large books of grants. While grants are commonly offered for college and vocational schooling, some are simply offered to qualified applicants and attending school is not a requirement. Most of these grants are offered by private foundations and some of the grants are quite obscure. For example, there may be a grant offered for a female of Italian descent who is between the ages of 18 and 45. If you meet those requirements, however, it is often quite easy to get that particular grant. Not all of the grants are so specific. Some of them are for categories of people. An example of this would be a grant for offspring of military personnel, offspring of civil service workers, offspring of graduates of a particular college, offspring of people who work for specific companies, people of a specific religious faith or people who have parents who belong to a service club or religious club. The list goes on and on. There are literally thousands of grants that go unclaimed each year. The only way to find out if there might be a grant for which you would qualify is to actually go to the library and pore over the grant books.

Government Grants

The United States government offers grants for specific categories of inventions. **The National Institute of Standards and Technology** offers funding for industrial and academic research in a variety of ways. For example, they fund proposals by small businesses for research and development efforts that fall within areas recommended yearly by the U.S. Department of Commerce. Find out if your business might qualify by calling (301) 975-3085. Or, for example, if your invention relates to fire prevention, you may qualify for the fire research grant. If you have a fire prevention product, contact Wanda Duffin at (301) 975-6863. You can find the complete list of grants offered by NIST at:

www.nist.gov/public_affairs/grants.htm

Other departments of the U.S. government also offer grants. The Energy Department and the Department of Homeland Security are examples of these. They are not the only departments of the U.S. government that offer grants, however. Contact the appropriate government department for your category of invention to see if there may be grants for which you would qualify.

Student inventors may qualify for special funding opportunities if they enter and win various student invention competitions. Information on those programs can be found at:

www.inventors.about.com/od/competitionsprize

Funding Option of Last Resort!

If none of these resources will work for you there is one final option. If you have valuables such as jewelry, antiques or stocks that are not a part of your retirement portfolio, and you are willing to part with them in order to fund your invention, you can sell them. We would only recommend this course of action if you have no other. Exhaust all other possibilities before selling off your valuables.

You can see that while there is funding available for Shoestring Budget™ inventors, there is no magic panacea. It is, instead, a common sense approach to creative ways to fund your invention. You can help to make up for limited funds by careful planning and cautious use of your limited resources.

CHAPTER NINE

Protecting Your Invention
What Will It Cost?

Patent Expenses

Probably the biggest blow to your budget will come in protecting your invention with a patent. Even in this very important area, there are ways to save money. For most new inventors, determining what your patent protection for your new product will cost is a shadowy area that is difficult to pin down. While we cannot give you exact figures, we can help you to determine approximately what you might need to budget for the protection of your invention.

Patents, Trademarks & Copyrights

In this book, we will only be discussing U. S. protection for your intellectual property. If you are interested in obtaining protection for your invention outside the U.S., most intellectual property attorneys should be able to help you with that. Often, new inventors are confused about the different types of intellectual property protection offered by the governments of the United States and other countries. We are sometimes asked, "Should I get a patent, a trademark, or a copyright?" Before we go any further, we will provide the definition of each of the three basic types of protection available for intellectual property. This definition comes from the USPTO's website.

"Patents, Trademarks, and Copyrights are three types of intellectual property protection. They are different and serve different purposes. Patents protect inventions, and improvements to existing inventions. Trademarks include any word, name, symbol, or device, or any combination, used, or intended to be used in commerce to identify and distinguish the goods of one manufacturer or seller from goods manufactured or sold by others, and to indicate the source of the goods. Service marks include any word, name, symbol, device, or any combination, used, or intended to be used, in commerce, to identify and distinguish the services of one provider from services provided by others, and to indicate the source of the services. Copyrights protect literary, artistic, and musical works".

You can see from the foregoing definition that you may want more than one type of protection, depending on what your invention is, what you intend to call it, and how you wish to market it.

Now that you know about the different types of intellectual property protection offered by the U.S. government, you will need to decide which type of intellectual property protection best fits your invention and your plans to market your invention. If you plan to become the manufacturer and distributor of your new product, you will want to proceed with the best and strongest protection that you can obtain. In most cases, this will be a utility patent. If your plan is simply to sell all rights to your invention to another entity outright and be forever done with it, you will also want to get a good, strong patent in order to get the maximum price that buyers will pay for your invention. If you intend to allow another to either make or sell your invention under a license for a royalty, you have a few options that we will discuss below.

First, let's make sure that you understand the available patent options and what each of these options covers so that you can make an informed decision.

What is a Patent?

A United States patent represents a legally enforceable right to exclude others from making, using, or selling the invention described by the claims in the patent in the United States. A patent gives you the right to use the U.S. Federal court system to exclude others from making, using, or selling your invention. Neither the U.S. Patent Office nor any other entity will enforce your patent rights for you. It is up to the owner of the patent to bear the financial burden of enforcing the patent using legal means. However, knowledge of the existence of another's patent is a deterrent for most competitors. Few competitors will go to the expense of making and selling a product that is patented by another because they know that they are inviting a lawsuit.

The terms "Patent Pending" and "Patent Applied For" are used to inform the public that an application for a patent has been filed. Patent protection, the right to bring a lawsuit against an infringer of a patent, does not start until the actual grant of a patent. Until your patent issues, your invention is in the public domain and available for anyone to manufacture if disclosed to others without being covered by a confidentiality agreement. Having the terms "patent pending" or "patent applied for" on your product also serves as a deterrent for would-be competitors. But, be aware that marking an article as being protected by a patent, when it is not, is illegal and subject to penalty.

Most manufacturers are reluctant to put a product that is described in a patent pending application by someone else into production since the manufacturer of the product will be subject to a lawsuit to stop producing the product when the patent issues. It is not a smart business decision for manufacturers to invest in a product that the manufacturer will ultimately have to stop selling. It also would be an embarrassment for manufacturers to tell potential buyers that the product can no longer be supplied since it is now protected by a patent owned by another.

Patents are issued only on actual inventions. A patent generally cannot be obtained on an idea or a suggestion.

Design Patent or Utility Patent?

The USPTO defines a utility patent as a patent that is granted to the inventor or discoverer of any new and useful process, machine, article of manufacture, composition of matter, or any new useful improvement thereof.

A design patent is defined as a new, original, and ornamental design for an article of manufacture. If you need to protect the construction or operation of your invention you would want a utility patent. If you need to protect the new, ornamental design for your invention, you would want to obtain a design patent.

There is another type of patent, the plant patent, that is also available; but most new inventors are not seeking that type of patent, so plant patents are not discussed in this book. If you are interested in information on plant patents, please access the information on the USPTO website, www.uspto. gov.

Within the last few years the USPTO has begun issuing utility patents on business methods as well. One example of a patented business method is Amazon's one click to purchase system. Prior to the Amazon "one click" patent, online purchasers were required to click multiple times in order to make a purchase using the Internet. Amazon patented a business method which required only one click to make an online purchase from them. Some independent inventors are creating new ways of doing business, but this book is directed more toward the independent inventors with less technologically advanced inventions having physical properties.

Each type of patent has its own length of time during which it is in force. A utility patent that was granted on or after June 8, 1995, expires 20 years from its earliest effective U.S. filing date. A design patent's term is 14 years from the date it was granted.

If your plan is to be your own manufacturer, either by making the product yourself or by having it manufactured, applying for the patent and then enforcing the patent against infringers will probably be your sole responsibility. You will want to get your patent application filed as soon as you are comfortable that you can market your invention. This will be important to you because you will want the exclusivity that a patent provides. Your decision at this point then becomes who will write, file, and prosecute your application? You have several choices:

Who Should Write Your Patent Application?

1. Patent Attorney- Patent attorneys, who generally call themselves intellectual property attorneys, are both licensed to practice law and registered to practice before the USPTO. This means that they can file and prosecute your patent application all the way through to the eventual issuance of the patent. Patent attorneys can render legal opinions about patents and can also represent you in court if there is litigation regarding your patent at any point. Any attorney can file a trademark registration application for you while only patent counsel, either patent attorneys or patent agents, can file and prosecute patent applications.

 Patent attorneys are likely to be the most expensive way to file a utility patent application, however if you can afford this option you can have a comfort level that you and your potential patent protection are in the most qualified of hands.

2. Patent Agent- This patent professional is also qualified to write and prosecute a patent application. Patent agents must pass the very same examination that is required of patent attorneys in order to practice before the USPTO. They are just as qualified as a patent attorney to prepare, file and prosecute patent applications. Patent agents are not able to represent you in court in the event of patent infringement litigation. However, the rates of patent agents may be less than those a patent attorney would charge. In the event that you would need to avail yourself of the services of an attorney later on, you can still do so.

You do not need to pay for formal patent drawings until you receive the Notice of Allowance from the USPTO. You may submit informal drawings until that time. Also, it is not necessary to get your formal drawings done through your patent attorney or patent agent. The patent attorney or patent agent will probably hire a professional patent draftsman and inflate the price to you in the process. You can save money by cutting out the middleman and hiring a professional patent draftsman directly at the time you actually need the formal drawings, not before.

3. Write and File Your own Patent Application- This is a risky practice because the techniques involved in patent claim drafting require the use of specialized terms and phrasing. But, for those who simply cannot afford to hire a patent professional, there are some aids available to assist you with the preparation and prosecution of your own patent application. There are books written by patent attorneys to teach the novice inventor how to write his own patent application. Probably the best book on this subject is **Patent It Yourself**, by attorney **David Pressman**. This book is written in easily understandable language and it includes all the legal forms an independent inventor could possibly need. It also includes suggestions for evaluating and marketing your invention. The book is from Nolo Press and it is widely available. At this writing, the cost is less than $40 through the **Nolo website**:

www.nolo.com

Patent it Yourself is also available through most public library systems, new and used bookstores as well as in the libraries of many independent inventor clubs and organizations.

Also available are special software packages designed to lead the inventor through the writing of a patent application. The best-known software for writing a utility patent is **PatentPro**. It was developed by **Robert Mason**, a Dallas, Texas, patent attorney. You can find out about it at:

www.patentpro.us

PatentPro allows the inventor to submit his completed application to a patent attorney for review as a part of the cost of the program. At the time of this writing, the cost of this software is under $300. You will find a coupon for a discount on this software in the coupon pages in the back of this book.

Another software package designed to assist the novice inventor in writing his own utility patent application is **PatentEase**. PatentEase costs about the same amount as **PatentPro** and you can get information on this software at:

www.patent-application.net

Even though these guides are designed to be used by independent inventors, you should be prepared to spend some time becoming familiar with these aids if you wish to follow this route. Come to think of it, any route you follow when writing your own application will require a great deal of your time. But, it may be worth it to you if you truly cannot afford to have your patent professionally written.

4. Write it Yourself with Assistance- Some patent professionals will agree to look over the patent application that you have written for accuracy and completeness for a fee that is far less than if they had written the application. This "hybrid" approach to getting your application written works well for independent inventors who cannot afford to have the application entirely written and filed by a patent attorney or a patent agent. Be aware that if you elect to use this option the prosecution of the application (dealing with the USPTO examiners) will be your responsibility. But, if you take this route, the patent professional who oversees your original application may be willing to assist you with office actions from the USPTO for an additional fee.

All of the above options for writing your own patent application are offered simply to inform you of what is available if you must write your own patent application. We are not offering an opinion as to the efficacy of the products for your particular situation. Please do your own due diligence on any product or method that you are considering for your very important protection.

Provisional U.S. Patent Applications

There is another inexpensive option that allows a measure of temporary protection and it has several uses for the independent inventor. We are speaking of the Provisional Patent Application. While it is referred to as an application, this document, which is simply filed away by the USPTO, will not be read by an examiner and, of itself, it will never result in a patent being issued. In fact, a Provisional Patent Application really isn't an application for anything. There is no published USPTO document entitled a Provisional Patent. How, then does the filing of a Provisional Patent Application benefit the Shoestring Budget™ inventor? There are some important things that a Provisional Patent Application can do for you.

1. You can easily prepare and file this document yourself, without the assistance of a patent professional.

2. From the moment you drop your Provisional U.S. Patent Application into the mail, you can be legally "patent pending" and can refer to your product as such.

3. The date that you mail the provisional patent application becomes the priority date for your utility patent application if you file a non-Provisional Patent Application within one year claiming the benefits of your earlier filing of a Provisional U.S. Patent Application.

4. If you license your invention during the year after filing your provisional application, your licensee may be willing to file for and pay for the eventual non-provisional utility patent application that will belong to you.

5. If you plan to build a business around the invention, a provisional patent application will provide a year of being "patent pending" while you see if the product has a market. If you find that it does not have a market, God forbid!, you will have cut your losses substantially by not having filed for the utility patent.

6. A provisional patent application costs only $100 to file at this writing. You can include more than one invention idea in the same Provisional Patent Application for that single fee.

We have stated that you can write your own Provisional Patent Application. The USPTO has a website that explains the program in detail at:

www.uspto.gov/web/offices/pac/provapp.htm

You will find the cover sheet for this application as a pdf document at:

www.uspto.gov/web/forms/sb0016.pdf

After carefully reading the instructions you will find on the first website listed above, print the cover sheet that is provided at the second website. Then, be sure to include a complete description of your invention, along with drawings, graphics and/or photos. The initial fee for filing a provisional application ($100 at this writing) allows up to 100 pages of material. For each 50 pages after the first 100, there is an additional fee of $125.

Now that we have told you some of the advantages of a Provisional Patent Application, here are a couple of caveats:

1. Provisional U.S. Patent Applications are only to be used for a product for which you would eventually file for a utility patent. Provisional U.S. Patent Applications are not for product designs.

2. For a utility patent to be issued from a provisional patent application, a non-provisional application must be filed within one year, claiming the benefit of the earlier filed provisional application.

A software product, **Patent Wizard**, is available that you can use for writing provisional applications if you do not choose to write it entirely on your own or to pay a patent professional to do it for you. This software was developed by patent attorney **Michael S. Neustel**. At this writing, the cost for the **Patent Wizard** software is $249 and it is available for downloading at:

www.patentwizard.com

There is also an excellent book that can help you to write a provisional patent application. It is **Patent Pending in 24 Hours** by attorneys **Richard Stim and David Pressman**. This paperback book is also available from Nolo Press or from your local library or bookstore.

Costs for Professional Services

Utility Patent

How do you determine what it will cost if you wish to hire a professional for your utility patent? We have obtained some ballpark ranges from several patent professionals to give you a feel for what your patent might cost. The cost of obtaining a good, strong utility patent can have a wide range, based on such variables as the complexity of the invention itself, the amount of prior art involved, and the number and complexity of the Office Action responses required. Each time you receive a letter from the patent office, taking some official action on your application, this is referred to as an Office Action. Obviously, if your invention is highly technical, it will require more of the patent professional's time to write the application. If there are a large number of similar products or patents, it will likewise require more work to prepare the patent application. And, when the patent examiner returns the application for changes in the claims, there is a charge each time for handling the response.

 Independent inventors, small businesses and non-profit organizations are entitled to what is known as small entity status. This qualifies you for reduced filing and maintenance fees, usually half of the cost for large entities.

We were quoted prices of $6,000-$11,000 for the initial writing and filing of a simple to moderately complex utility patent application. These fees may or may not include costs such as filing fees, petition fees, drawings and handling fees. Your initial fee could be more or less than this range, depending on the professional that you choose, the area of the United States where the attorney or agent works, and whether they work independently or with a large firm, etc.

No matter what the initial fee is, you will not be required to come up with additional money until the first Office Action comes from the USPTO. This is not likely to occur for a year or longer, so you will have time to accumulate the money to pay for the response to that Office Action.

Your attorney's or agent's responses to the Office Actions will typically cost $2,500 for a response to the first Office Action and about $1,500 for a response to the second Office Action (if a second one is necessary). At this writing, the utility patent issue fee is $700 and your attorney or agent may add in his own fee for handling. Utility patents will have maintenance fees payable in six month windows which open at of 3 , 7 , and 11 years after the date the patent is granted, ranging from $450-$1,900 at this writing (based on which maintenance fee is being paid). Again, these are the USPTO fees and your attorney may charge a bit more for handling the payment of maintenance fees for you.

Did you know that many patent attorneys do not charge for your first visit with them? Often patent attorneys provide this initial consultation to you as a community service to help you determine if you should apply for patent protection. This is a freebie that can be worth a lot of money, considering that attorney fees can be as much as $300-$500 per hour! Call around to find an attorney who provides this service. And, when you make that first visit with an attorney, it is perfectly acceptable to ask what the charge will be for writing and filing your patent application.

Design Patent

These often-misunderstood patents aren't even called patents in other countries. They are called "industrial designs registrations" or "utility models registrations" and are more closely akin to trademarks in that their value lies solely in protecting the appearance of something, rather than its function. Appearance can be very valuable in certain contexts, such as tire treads, sport shoes and even such readily recognizable items as the shape of the Coca Cola® bottle. As such, design patent applications cost considerably less simply because the preparation and prosecution of design patent applications is less involved.

Typical costs for a design patent range from $1,000-$4,000 from filing all the way through prosecution to issuance. A large part of this amount can be attributed to draftsman's fees. Obviously, the cost will vary according to the number of drawings included. Unfortunately, the law describing the process of applying for a design patent is inflexible so that, if the examiner rejects a design patent application based on a prior art reference, there is very little you can do to amend an application for a design patent.

Issue fees for design patents are $400 at this writing, plus the attorney's handling charge. Design patents do not incur maintenance fees, as do utility patents.

Trademarks

Trademarks do not have to be registered to obtain rights to prevent others from using the same or a similar trademark, but federal registration significantly enhances these rights in a trademark. You can claim exclusive rights to use your trademark, after you have searched the USPTO's database to be certain that it is available, simply by putting the symbol ™ after your product name each and every time you use it. It costs nothing to do this and it provides notice to others of your claim to this trademark. It is not a federally registered trademark, however. A trademark registration can be obtained from both the state and federal governments. If a product/service is going to be sold across state lines . . . think Internet sales . . . then a federal trademark registration should be obtained. The cost for having a law firm prepare and prosecute a trademark registration application varies according to the number of classes in which the goods and services are to be registered. We were quoted prices averaging from $1,000 to $3,000 to obtain a federal trademark registration. But the cost can be higher depending upon the existence of similar trademarks. There are no maintenance fees for federal trademarks but federal trademark registrations must be renewed every ten years. Renewal cost at this time is around $500.

If you have not yet used your trade or service mark, you can file an Intent to Use trademark registration application. The typical cost for an attorney to write and file your Intent to Use Trademark Registration Application is about $500, but it is very simple for the Shoestring Budget™ inventor to do this for himself online and the cost at this writing is about $325 if the intent to use trademark registration application is filed electronically.

A trademark application may be for only one mark (the trademark itself), but the application can have multiple classes (different designations for the mark, such as the use of the name Coca Cola® on both cookie jars and on Christmas decorations). At this writing, the filing fee for a trademark is $325 per class if filed electronically. The trademark side of the USPTO encourages online filing by offering reduced fees for filing electronically rather than filing a paper application. Specifically, you can reduce the filing fee for a trademark registration application by about $50 per class by filing online. Additionally, some special conditions will allow you to obtain an even lower filing fee of $275 per class. Find out about those conditions and if you can take advantage of them at:

www.uspto.gov/web/offices/com/sol/notices/70fr38768.pdf

The USPTO offers three options for payment when filing online: credit card, automatic deposit account, and electronic funds transfer. Find out about these options at:

www.uspto.gov/teas/payment.htm

 Since we are primarily dealing with cost issues in this book, if you intend to file for your own trademark registration online, you will need to make use of the detailed information you will find at:

www.uspto.gov/main/trademarks.htm

Copyrights

Copyrights, since they are not used to protect inventions, will not be dealt with here except to say that as intellectual property protection they do deserve a mention. Copyright registration applications are not handled by the USPTO; rather, copyright registrations are granted by the **U.S. Copyright Office** at:

www.copyright.gov

The U. S. Copyright Office is a division of the Library of Congress. Basic copyright registration fees are very reasonable, starting at around $30 and it is a very simple matter to obtain a federal copyright registration without assistance.

The price ranges in this chapter are offered only for you to get a feel for the general amount of money you might need for each of the intellectual property protection options. The price ranges may vary widely, based on the factors mentioned in the chapter, but the foregoing discussion provides a ballpark idea of what your costs will be if you have determined exactly what protection you will need to obtain. Just remember: Don't be afraid to ask whomever you approach, right upfront, about what the costs and payment options will be for the assistance they can offer you. A clear understanding on both sides will smooth the way for a positive experience.

Remember also that of all the phases of your product development, the protection or your protectable intellectual property is arguably the most important to you in terms of your future profits. The money you spend on getting the best protection you can get will likely come back to you many times over.

CHAPTER TEN

Now What?
License It or Start a Business?

Decisions, Decisions!

Almost from the moment you conceived your great idea, you were probably thinking of a future for the product you would create. Maybe you were dreaming of building a company around it and creating a new career. Perhaps you were thinking of adding it as a new product to a company you already operate. On the other hand, you might have been thinking, as more and more independent inventors do these days, of licensing the invention to a manufacturer for a royalty from the sales of the product. Maybe you just aren't sure how you want to proceed. Let's look at the options and you can decide what works best for you.

Remember that there is no right or wrong option for product developers. The right option is the one that fits your product, your situation and your lifestyle. Independent inventors have made huge successes (and huge flops!) in every marketing option. It pays to think it through carefully before making this major decision.

Should you manufacture your own product?

If you can simply add the new product because it fits right in with your existing business, this is probably the easiest and least expensive route for you. This often happens because a business owner creates a product that presents a better way to do a job or offer a service that is already a part of his business. If the new product works for him, it should work for his customers as well. He has only to do his research, obtain legal protection for the product, and make it known to his customers.

Difficulties of being your own manufacturer/distributor

If you currently do not have a business and it is your desire to build a business around your invention, you can do it, but it becomes a much more risky proposition. In the example above, the business owner can lose some money if the product fails, but he is not likely to lose the entire business unless he has risked the company's stability on the success of that product. If you choose to build an entire business around a new product, not only will you need a substantial amount of start up capital, including enough to survive until the company becomes self-sustaining, you will need to be virtually certain of the success of the product.

There are some astounding success stories of people who have built profitable businesses around a single product. It can happen. But, the odds against huge successes with businesses built around a single product seem to be getting steeper. One important reason is that the buyers for the major retailers will not even allow single-product vendors an appointment to show their product to them.

If you have only one product to sell to a major retail chain, you are not likely to be given that opportunity, no matter how great your product may be. While the retail stores are made to look cheerful with bright colors, bright lighting and background music to enhance the shopping experience, to the retailer it is very serious business and each inch of shelf space is allotted to a particular manufacturer in a map of the store, known as a planogram. Getting your product on that planogram is not an easy task if you have but one product.

Product Representatives

One option to get around this problem, if you plan to manufacture and distribute your own product, is to place your product with an independent product representative. This is a person who represents a number of products from various manufacturers to the retailers. Be aware, if you do this, that you will have to pay the product representative a percentage of the sales for this representation. This can make a significant difference in your profit bottom line, but it may be the only way that you can get your product into the large retail chains.

You can find product representatives by contacting administrative offices of the retail stores and asking them for the names of the reps for your category of products. Product representatives usually cover a specific geographic region. For example, there may be a product representative who covers Texas, Oklahoma and Louisiana. The entire country is divided into exclusive regions for the individuals representing specific lines of products. This approach may require you to contact product representatives all over the country in order to get maximum market coverage for your product, but it can work.

In addition to individual product representatives, for many categories of products there are distributors. These are companies that handle the distribution of an entire category of products to select retailers. When we were marketing **Ghostline®** on our own, before licensing the product, we sold some product to a distributor who got **Ghostline®** into stores in a seven-state area. This involved another layer of wholesaling (from us to the distributor and from the distributor to the retailer), but if your profit margin is great enough, you can get greater distribution this way.

You can often find lists of Product Representatives and Distributors in the back of the business directories that can be found in the business department of your local library. You may be amazed to find that there are professional directories for virtually every sector of the market. You will feel as if you have struck gold when you locate the professional directory for your category of product. It will include manufacturers with all their contact information as well as product representatives and product distributors.

 If you plan to be your own manufacturer and deal with retail buyers, learn the language of retailing and be prepared to talk about such things as "planograms," "sku numbers, " and "upc codes" in order to understand and be understood.

Other things to consider if your goal is to be the manufacturer of your product:

A. Will you maintain manufacturing facilities and hire the work done or import your product.

B. Will you hire a sales force, place the product with a product representative and/or a distributor, or be your own salesperson.

C. Will you handle the day-to-day requirements of running the business.

There are both advantages and disadvantages to building a business around your invention. You are the only one who is in a good position to decide whether that is the correct choice for you. It will depend in large part on your current financial situation, your age, your state of health, and how you want to spend your time. If you have the financial ability, the expertise and you are up for the challenge, maybe this is the route for you. If being in control of your product is important to you, then this may be the right option for you. You can certainly exercise total control over your product when you are the manufacturer.

 Be aware that if you are the manufacturer and distributor of your product, you will be responsible for providing product liability insurance to the retailers who sell the product. All retail products,

no matter how innocuous they appear to be, must carry product liability insurance.

If you are building a business around your invention, keep in mind that it is your responsibility to enforce your patent. If you should find your product infringed this could be a significant expense. Many independent inventors choose to license their products for this reason alone. They know that they would never have the financial resources to sue for infringement. Large companies also know that small independent product developers are not likely to have the funds to force them to stop if they choose to infringe. This makes it more likely that a large company might consider it worth the relatively small risk that an independent inventor could make them stop producing and selling the inventor's patent protected product.

Catalogs

There is yet another route that some inventors take with their inventions and sometimes this one works for those who have a good idea for a product that cannot be patent protected because it is already in the public domain. That is, the product or something very similar has already been patented or sold before, but it is still a viable product.

You are not required to get a patent if you choose not to do so. If protection from competition is not important to you and the product is not currently covered by an existing patent, you can simply market the product in whatever way you choose. If the product is a really good one, you will probably not maintain exclusivity for a very long time, but if you think yours may be a fad-type product, it could be a wise decision to just get on the market with it and make your profit while the fad lasts.

Catalogs often sell items that have no patents. It is relatively easy to get your product into catalogs if you are willing to manufacture and sell it to the catalog companies. If you are interested in this option, just go online and check with the catalog or catalogs of your choice. They all have contact information. Contact them and let them know that you are interested in submitting a product for their catalog. They will send you their submission requirements.

Television shopping channels & infomercials

If you want to manufacture your product with the goal of selling it on one of the television shopping channels, you can find out about their requirements by going online to their websites. If they select your product for televising, you will need to provide them with a large amount of the product, so you will have to be financially prepared to handle that. Be aware that if you sell product to the shopping networks, they have the option of sending it back to you if it doesn't sell, so you may need a backup plan for the merchandise.

Another option you may want to check out is the growing popularity of infomercials. If you are reading this book, you probably don't have the thousands of dollars it normally takes to get an infomercial filmed and to buy the television airtime. There is another way to get an infomercial, if you have a product that is patent-protected and enticing enough to grab the attention of an infomercial marketer. Some legitimate companies will take your product, produce the advertising and pay for the airtime in exchange for a hefty percentage of the profits. Notice that we said, "some legitimate companies." There are also many scams in this particular industry, so be very careful here.

Independent inventors are often so in love with their invention ideas that they are easy prey for crooks who tell them that they will take their wonderful invention and make them overnight millionaires. If they are asking for a large sum of money from you in order to give you this wonderful infomercial deal, head for the door. The truly legitimate ones put their own money into the projects.

License your product?

Another option that many independent inventors are choosing nowadays is to license their inventions for royalties. This is a method of choice for many inventors for lots of compelling reasons. Once a product is licensed to a manufacturer, that product will automatically have a place on the planogram of the retail stores where the manufacturer places goods. The manufacturers handle all of the responsibility for producing the product, selling it to retailers, bookkeeping, etc. The licensor (the inventor) goes to his mailbox and collects his royalty checks at regular intervals, usually quarterly. The inventor's time is entirely his own to spend creating other moneymaking new products or in whatever way he chooses.

While receiving a royalty amount of 3-5 percent of net sales on your product may seem like settling for a very small amount, consider this: the manufacturer is taking all of the financial risk in getting the product on the market. He is spending the money to make the product, warehouse it, insure it, sell it, ship it and handle the bookkeeping. His profit margin on the product may not be as great as you imagine. In addition, if you have a guaranteed annual amount of royalty (and you should!) you will receive at least that amount whether your licensee sells that much of your product or not. Lest you jump to the conclusion that 3-5 percent of the wholesale price does not amount to much, do the math. A product that retails $8-$10 million annually returns between $120,000 and $250,000 in royalty, depending on the percentage. This is money that you didn't lift a finger to earn once it was licensed. If you are still thinking 3-5 percent is a paltry amount of royalty, consider this; if you are unable to get the product marketed on your own, 3-5 percent of something is much to be preferred over 100 percent of nothing!

 It is important to know that most large manufacturers will not sign your non-disclosure documents, but they will insist on your signing their submission documents before you can submit your

invention to them. You will have to be willing to do this if you wish to submit your invention to them for licensing consideration.

If you have decided on licensing as your option, there are some things you will need to know before you go out to contact manufacturers. The first and most important thing is that manufacturers have no reason to pay for an unprotected product. It would make no sense for them to commit to pay you a royalty if their competition could immediately begin making and selling a similar product. If they are ethical, and most of them are, manufacturers won't even look at your invention until you have taken some protective steps.

Most of the larger manufacturers will require you to sign their submission documents before they will look at your information. These documents are designed to protect the manufacturer against an individual's claiming that the company took his idea. The submission documents usually state that by signing them you are aware that they may have already seen, been working on or previously rejected the same or a similar idea. If you want to move forward with them you must sign these forms.

 Submission forms that you send to manufacturers can also be considered part of your "paper trail" of proof that you disclosed your invention to them should you ever need it. Be sure to keep copies of everything in your files.

If the company is not ethical and you show your unprotected invention or idea to them, they can simply take it. Therefore, the thing to remember is to make sure that you have carefully followed your early protective procedures before approaching anyone regarding licensing. They protect themselves and you should do likewise.

How to find potential licensees

Product Labels & Packaging

How do you find the company that might become your licensee? There are several ways and you begin gathering that information at the beginning of your invention process. This is all part of research that you will be doing anyway and it costs you nothing. While you are doing your market searching to make sure that your idea is not already on the store shelves, you will be looking in stores at merchandise that is in the same category as your idea. For example, if your idea is for a sporting goods product, you will be looking in the sporting goods department of discount stores and in sporting goods specialty stores. When you are looking at items that are similar or in the same category as your invention, look at the labels on those items. You will find the name of the manufacturer and sometimes you will find web addresses and phone numbers. You will find this same type of information with your Internet and catalog research. Begin keeping a file of this information. These are possible licensees for your product.

Patent Assignees

When you begin your online preliminary patent searching (see Chapter 4), as you look at patents in the USPTO database, you will notice that some of the patents have been assigned to a manufacturer. This is sometimes the case when an employee of that manufacturer developed the product in-house and the patent automatically belongs to the company. Sometimes an independent inventor developed and patented the item and assigned it to the company. Either way, that company is a potential licensee for you. Put them on your list.

Library Reference Department

Yet another way to find potential licensees is to visit the reference department of your public library and look in the Thomas Register, a set of

20 reference books that lists most of the manufacturers in the United States. This set of directories lists these companies in a number of different ways and has a wealth of information about them. This research method can help you to find companies you might not otherwise have known about if you didn't run across their products in your store and Internet searching. You can also access the Thomas Register online but if you are unfamiliar with it, you may not find everything you need online. In our experience, you can find a lot more information by looking in the actual books. The reference librarian at your public library can help you to find all of the different types of information that is in these directories. There are other directories of manufacturers at the library also and you may find one that is specific to the industry you are targeting.

Public libraries are available online and most of them have business databases, such as Reference USA, on which they pay subscription fees, but they make them available for free to library card holders. This is another way to locate potential licensees from your home computer.

Trade Shows

Yet another great way to find manufacturers is to attend a trade show. This is where you will not only find all of the major players in the industry of your choice under one roof, but you will be able to look at their booths and get a good idea of what their product lines look like. Sometimes it is difficult to get a feel for a manufacturer from one or two products on a store shelf, but when you see their booth adjacent to those of their competitors and all of their products displayed, you get a better idea about the company.

Trade shows do not normally charge admission to attend. But, admission to trade shows is usually restricted to those within the industry. In most cases, it is not too difficult to get into them. Sometimes gaining entrance to these trade shows is simply a matter of visiting with the manager of your neighborhood retail store who might be attending and asking him to allow you to attend as his guest. Members are usually allowed to bring guests for a one or two-day pass. Going as the guest of a retailer does not mean that you have to be there in the actual presence of that retailer. They usually just issue a guest nametag to you and you can attend at your own convenience.

If you cannot find a retailer who can get you in, call the number that you will find listed online for the tradeshow and ask about the admission requirements. Sometimes an associate membership is an inexpensive way to become an instant "insider." In addition to gaining entrance to tradeshows, an associate membership entitles you to the organization's membership directory; a listing of all of its members, separated by product category, and contact information for each member. This is something that may be worth the price of a membership in itself.

If you cannot afford to buy an associate membership in the association that is sponsoring the trade show or if you don't meet the qualifications to become an associate member (but being a product developer usually meets the membership requirement), you may decide to get creative. By this, we mean that we have heard of inventors who gained entrance to trade shows by printing business cards that indicated their association with a small retail store and then they showed a business check with a generic-sounding name. They were given nametags and ushered inside! We are not recommending this option; we are simply stating that we are aware that it is sometimes done. However, it is usually not necessary to go to these lengths to gain admission to a trade show.

If you have a product that is patent protected and ready to present for licensing you may be tempted to rent a small booth at a trade show to display your product. Resist this temptation. The manufacturers you want to reach are busy running their own booths and they seldom, if ever, get around to visiting all of the other booths at these large trade shows. What you want to do is learn about all of your potential licensees and leave your business card with them.

The purpose of these trade shows is for the manufacturers to make sales to the retail buyers and this is what they will be concentrating on for the first couple of days of the show. If you attempt to talk to them during their busy time, you will only anger them and hurt your case. But, here is the secret . . . go on the last day of the trade show. By then the buyers have come and gone and the manufacturers are just waiting to break down those booths and return to their home offices. They are bored and willing to talk with anyone who comes by. It is still to your advantage to keep it short. Just introduce yourself, pick up their business card and hand them one of yours. Ask if they license products from outside product developers. Be sure to refer to yourself as a product developer and not an inventor. Calling yourself an inventor is a red flag that you are new at marketing products. You can tell them that you have a newly patented (or patent-pending) product that is a perfect fit for their product line and you will contact them for an appointment within a week or so. This is all you need to do at this point. Smile, shake hands with them and leave. Don't wear out your welcome.

Resist the urge to take your prototype to the trade show, no matter how good it looks, and don't tell the booth attendants exactly what your product is. If they ask, and they might, just tell them that it is "an improved widget" or "a solution to the problem of ___." Some eager inventors have lost their opportunities at trade shows by giving away too much too soon!

After you are out of their sight, make notes so that you will remember them and their product line and you are ready to contact them a couple of weeks later.

Most manufacturers scan visitors' business cards into their computers at trade shows, so if you give them your business card you can be sure that they will still have it available to them when you phone them later. And, if you call the number that is on their business card, rather than the published number for the company, you are likely to reach the desk of the exact person with whom you wish to speak.

Whatever method you decide to pursue for the marketing of your invention, keep your eye out and you will find ways to save money at every step along the way. After all, you are a very creative person!

CHAPTER ELEVEN

From Inventing To Marketing:
Changing Gears

Moving to the Next Phase!

Many independent inventors develop their ideas, create working prototypes of their ideas, file for or obtain their patent protection for their inventions, and then stop, frozen in inactivity, because they mistakenly think that manufacturers will hear of their inventions and seek them out, eager to license their newly patented products. Unfortunately, that isn't the way it works in the real world. Too many people believe that old quote by Ralph Waldo Emerson, "Build a better mousetrap and the world will beat a path to your door." If that old saying was ever true, it is no longer true. In an effort to be as cost efficient as possible most manufacturers and companies are working with as few employees as possible. The economy no longer allows for employee-heavy companies. Companies are downsizing rather than adding redundant employees. As a result, their employees are busy operating and growing the companies in their existing markets rather than exploring new markets. They may welcome new patent protected products that are presented to them if they fit in with their existing line of products and existing distribution channels, but most do not have the manpower to actively seek out new inventions. They do not have someone who has the time to peruse through new patents that have been issued to see if they might find something that would benefit their company.

Present Your Product Yourself

There are, of course, professional licensing agents you can hire to present your product to manufacturers for possible licensing; but if you are a Shoestring Budget™ inventor, and you must be if you are reading this book, we are going to tell you how to do it yourself, for the bare minimum of costs. Actually, in many ways, it is an advantage for you, the actual inventor (product developer), to present your product for licensing to manufacturers. As the developer, you know your product and its benefits better than anyone else does. Your enthusiasm for your product will be apparent when you meet with potential licensees. Let your enthusiasm for your product show! If you go in to your appointment with the possible licensee and you appear nervous, apprehensive or tentative about your product, your chances of inspiring them to be enthusiastic about it are very slim. If, on the other hand, you go in enthusiastic and excited about how perfect your product is for their company and how it will fit perfectly into their product line, your enthusiasm will be infectious. Infect them! Tell them why it makes sense, economically, for them to license your invention. Tell them why and how your product will make money for them.

You'll notice that at this point we are talking about how your product will help the manufacturer, not the end user. From the time when you first dreamed up your great idea, you were, undoubtedly, thinking of how the end user of your product would benefit from it. That is natural. We all think that way because inventing is solving a problem we have; or creating a better, easier, or more cost efficient way of doing something. Inventing is solving real problems for real people, just like us. Although it is obviously important that you keep the end user of your product in mind, when the time comes to license your product, your customer is no longer the end user; your customer is now the manufacturer. You must convince the manufacturer that your product makes sense for this particular company. You must present compelling reasons why this company should license your product. The bottom line is what is important to manufacturers. Your product presentation must make a strong case that your product will make money for them and you must have the facts and figures to back up your claims.

Getting Attention for Your Product

You have kept your invention pretty much under wraps until now. And you may elect to continue with the secrecy if your patent has not yet issued. But, if you are going to license your product to a manufacturer, you will want to "blow your horn" a bit now to this selected audience. One good way to do that is by sending out news releases announcing your wonderful new product.

The news release that we are recommending is not targeted toward the news media, but toward the specific manufacturers you wish to attract. The news release will be written exactly as a press release would be written but it will be sent in a special way to the manufacturers. By this, we mean that you will not simply fax or mail it to them. Manufacturers receive huge amounts of mail daily so it is necessary for your news release to stand out from the crowd. How do you do that? By making sure it arrives by messenger, either UPS, Federal Express or some other special delivery method. Even though it costs more to have your mail delivered by messenger, your package that is delivered in this way immediately moves to the top of the pile. Often, unsolicited mail that arrives in the usual way is discarded unopened. Personalized delivery ensures that your mail will be opened.

Once your special delivery is opened, and it is determined that it is unsolicited, it is important to have a headline that will grab attention so that it will not be routinely discarded. Jeff Crilley, Emmy Award winning newscaster for Dallas' Fox Television Channel, says to think of it as if you were writing a headline for a newspaper. Make the headline say something that might even have shock value. We don't mean that you should take a tip from the tabloids and make a ridiculous statement. Rather, you should focus on the most unique thing about your invention. Maybe your headline could be something about you, the inventor, and the frustration that caused you to create the product. Or, perhaps it could be a startling headline about someone using your product. As an example, on the following page is a news release for a new product that makes it possible to actually play a piano or other keyboard instrument without knowing how to read music.

 Get $5 dollars off the cover price of "Free Publicity" by using the discount coupon in the coupon section at the back of this book.

News Release example:

NEWS RELEASE

FOR IMMEDIATE RELEASE   CONTACT:
January 11, 2005   Bob Hulcher
                               Sales & Licensing

MAN PLAYS PIANO LIKE VIRTUOSO
INSTANTLY WITH NO TRAINING

The tinkling strains of "Smoke Gets in Your Eyes"
and the majestic swells of "How Great Thou Art"
waft from pianos that were previously gathering
dust in living rooms across America. Think there's
nothing unusual about that? Think again! The pian-
ists in these scenarios have never played piano and
do not read music! All this and much more are now
possible thanks to a brand new product.

The Pianomate®, a small device that sits atop the
keyboard with lights that show which keys to play,
makes it possible for anyone to play instantly,
with both hands, as if they knew how to read music.

Robert Hulcher, of Mobile, Alabama, the inventor of
Pianomate®, said, "I created this product because I
always wanted to play piano but I didn't want to
bother with all the tedium of learning to read
notes. I still can't read music, but I can certainly
play the piano!" The Pianomate® is designed to do
more than allow the user to play without reading
music. It also teaches note reading for those who
wish to use it as a learning tool in addition to
playing for pleasure.

Pianomate is available for purchase or for licensing.
Contact Robert Hulcher at (866) 532-7674. More information is available at www.pianomate.com.

You can write an attention-grabbing news release that will entice manufacturers to want to see your invention for themselves. All news releases follow the same format so, if you adhere to the format and think creatively, you can write a really good release that will showcase your invention. We will give you some hints below for following the format and you can refer back to the sample release to see how it was done.

All news releases have the same six basic parts, the banner head (title), dateline, contact, headline, first paragraph, and second (and sometimes third) paragraphs.

- The **Banner Head** is simply a title for your page: NEWS RELEASE (all caps).

- The **Dateline** lists when it is to be released: FOR IMMEDIATE RELEASE (all caps) and the date.

- **Contact information** comes next: CONTACT (all caps) and the name and title of the person to be contacted.

- **Headline**: Possibly the most important part of the document. See the shock value of the headline in the sample release above.

- **Paragraph One**: Think of it as the opening paragraph of a newspaper or magazine article and come up with an interesting way to begin the story. Describe the problem the invention solves and give a brief description of the product.

- **Paragraph Two**: Elaborate, use a quote from someone of importance to the story and give brief details about the fact that the product is available for exclusive licensing.

That's all there is to it! Practice a bit and you'll be writing news releases that manufacturers will find irresistible. This is the first step to getting serious attention from the exact people you wish to reach. It costs only a bit of your time and the delivery fee.

Meeting the Manufacturer

There are two components to your presentation, an oral component and a written component. The first part of your presentation is the oral component. If it is at all possible, you should travel to the manufacturer's offices and make your presentation in person. You may be saying to yourself, "But, I am too shy! I wouldn't feel comfortable in a corporate setting! I don't know how to do it!" In this chapter, we are going to demystify the process so that you will not only feel comfortable, you will even enjoy it!

Selecting the manufacturers to whom you will present your product is crucially important. Do your homework in advance so that you know before you ever call them that your product and their company are a good match. Don't waste your time or theirs in presenting your product to companies who do not have the distribution channels or manufacturing capabilities to market your invention.

The Oral Presentation

When you meet with the manufacturers to convince them to license your product, it is a business meeting and you will need to approach it as such. Dress appropriately. Wear business-appropriate clothing. Their first impression of you, the way you look and carry yourself, counts. Even if they are dressed more casually, you will command more respect and your product will be taken more seriously if you are dressed more formally. You are meeting with them as a professional product developer. They are comfortable meeting with other professionals and you must be professional in both your dress and your manner of speaking.

Always refer to yourself as a professional product developer, not an inventor. Product developers are professionals. Inventors are garage tinkerers who probably do not understand the realities of the business world. The word inventor often conjures up visions of a wild-eyed, wild-haired dreamer a la Doc in the "Back to the Future" movies.

Your meeting with the potential licensing manufacturer typically will last less than half an hour. The purpose of the meeting is to enthusiastically present your product and its many benefits in a concise and coherent manner that answers the questions manufacturers will have. Everyone likes a story. Begin your presentation by telling them how you came to create this product. Tell the manufacturer the problem you experienced and how your invention solves it. Tell them exactly what your invention is and how it works. Give the manufacturer the results of your research on the potential market size for your product. Explain how your product is a logical extension of the manufacturer's current product line. Give them facts and figures on the manufacturing costs as well as any special equipment that would be required in order to manufacture your product. Additionally, make the case for what the retail selling price of your product should be, as well as any documentation, market surveys or studies that you have done or had done, or actual sales records. In short, put yourself in the manufacturer's place and try to answer the questions you would have if you were the manufacturer.

Do not be intimidated by the people who hold important positions within the manufacturing company you have come to see. Remember that they are just like you, working people. They have an interest in what you have come to show them or you wouldn't have the appointment with them. Relax and show your enthusiasm for your new product and their company.

If it is possible, bring the prototype of your invention to the meeting. Manufacturers like to hold, touch, and examine the actual prototype. The more you can make the prototype look like an existing product in their product line, the better! Make sample packaging using their company logo and style. You can copy their company logo from their website for your mockup packaging. The easier you make it for the manufacturer to picture your product as a part of their product line, the easier it will be for them to make the decision to license it.

Finally, tell the manufacturer what you want. If you are looking to license your product, tell them so. If you are hoping to sell the rights to your patent outright, tell them. Too often, product developers will go to the meeting, present the product, and then fail to move the process forward by failing to tell the manufacturers what they want from them. We suggest that you take a sample license agreement with your name and their company name, and even with a suggested royalty rate, already filled in. Explain that the licensing agreement is simply a starting point for the negotiations. Most manufacturers appreciate your candor and upon reading the sample license agreement, the manufacturer will see that your requests are all reasonable. Any fears that the manufacturer may have that you have unreasonable expectations regarding potential income will be alleviated.

 Your meeting with the manufacturer should be fun, so don't forget to smile and look them in the eye! People often assume that someone who will not give them eye contact has something to hide. That is the last thing you wish for the manufacturer to assume.

The Written Presentation

The second part of your presentation is in written form. It is a 10-12 page booklet with questions the manufacturers will have and brief answers to those questions. The written presentation answers the questions you address in the face-to-face meeting, but it is a document that the manufacturers can keep after you have left that will explicitly outline the salient points of your oral presentation, and more. Your written presentation should not be given to the manufacturers until you have completed your oral presentation. Giving it to them in advance invites them to be looking through it rather than listening to you, your story and your enthusiasm about your product.

 Each time you write your product name, if you have not filed for federal trademark protection, always put the symbol ™ after it. You are allowed to claim the trademark in this way.

Your presentation should address each question the manufacturer will have in a succinct and clear manner. Do not include long pages of prose; it is unlikely that the manufacturer would ever read them. Answer the same questions you answered in your oral presentation. Tell them what your product is, how it works, what will be entailed in making it, who the potential market consists of and the size of that market, and what it will cost to manufacture the product as well as the likely retail selling price. If you have actually manufactured and sold the product, include documentation of your sales records. This is compelling proof that there is a market for your product and what the retail-selling price of the product might be. If you have done surveys of potential users of your product, include those. If you have done focus groups, include those. In short, use this presentation to give the manufacturer every reason to license your product.

Your written presentation serves three major purposes. First, it is a quick and easy reference on what your product is and how it makes economic sense for this manufacturer to license it. Second, the written presentation speaks on your behalf once you have gone. This important document can be used to present your product to decision makers within the company who were not at your meeting. Finally, if you are unable to meet with the potential licensing manufacturer in person, your written presentation is the next best thing to a face-to-face meeting. If you are unable to meet with the manufacturer in person, be certain to include with the presentation you submit, a cover letter explaining the story of your invention and how you came to invent it.

If you are unable to schedule a personal meeting with the manufacturer, it is important to maximize your chances that they will give your written presentation the attention it deserves by making it a compelling representation of your invention.

Do not ever send a written presentation without previously talking to someone at the company and getting the name of the appropriate person to whom it should be submitted.

Address your written presentation to a specific person within the potential licensing company and do not mail it standard U.S. mail. Send it by Express Mail, Federal Express, or UPS. Packages that arrive in one of these attention getting ways seem more important and make it more likely that the manufacturer will open and consider your submission. If it is possible, include a prototype of your invention with your written presentation.

Place your written presentation into an inexpensive vinyl folder or folio. This gives it a more businesslike appearance than a sheaf of papers held together by a paper clip or staple. The attractive professional folder will also make it easier for the manufacturer to identify and locate your written presentation at a later time.

Whether you meet with the potential licensing manufacturer in person or mail the written presentation to them, give the manufacturer at least three or four copies of your presentation. There may be multiple decision makers within the company who should have copies of your written presentation. Failure to send or give multiple copies can slow down the manufacturer's consideration process if one copy of the presentation has to be shared by several decision makers within the company. Additionally, there is always the chance that one person could inadvertently sabotage the entire consideration process if that person is simply too busy and he lets your presentation slip through the cracks. Multiple copies of the written presentation, in the hands of numerous decision makers within the potential licensing manufacturing company will help to keep your proposal active and your invention on the front burner.

Getting the Appointment

We have now discussed how to make your oral presentation and what should be in your written presentation, but we have not addressed how to make the call to get that all important appointment with the potential licensing manufacturer in the first place. There are definite dos and don'ts regarding the call to the manufacturer. First and most importantly, do your homework in advance so that you know the name and number of the appropriate person within the company to contact regarding your invention. If it is a small company, it may be the president. If it is a large company, it may be a vice-president in charge of product development or a member of the product development team.

Do not contact the president directly if it is a large company. Product development departments are very protective of their turf and will probably not be receptive to a product that circumvents their department. The NIH ("not invented here") disease has derailed many a good invention simply because the proper protocol was not followed when submitting the product. On the other hand, if you submit your product through the product development department and they adopt it as a 'find' they have acquired for the company, they are much more likely to promote and push your product through to licensing.

When you call for the appointment with the manufacturer, introduce yourself and ask for the appropriate person by name.

Then, when you get the appropriate person on the telephone, respect his time and his busy schedule. Introduce yourself as a professional product developer rather than an inventor. A generic name for your business, which could be any type of company, is helpful. For example, our company name is Second Sight Enterprises, Inc. Second Sight Enterprises, Inc. could be any type of business. When we call a manufacturer and introduce ourselves as product developers from a company called Second Sight Enterprises, Inc., they accept that we are a company of professional product developers.

If you do not have a company name, simply introduce yourself as a professional product developer. Always be truthful and don't ever try to bluff in this regard. If you should get discovered trying to bluff in something as unimportant as whether you actually represent a company, you could destroy your chances before you get to first base with them. Be yourself and be honest.

Explain that your company has developed a product that is a perfect match for the potential licensing manufacturer's line of products and distribution channels. The manufacturer will undoubtedly ask you what your product is. Don't tell them! If you describe your product at this point, it will give them the opportunity to dismiss your invention without giving it proper consideration. Instead, describe the problem your invention solves and request an appointment to demonstrate it for them in person.

The following is a sample script for your telephone call:

Louise: *Hello, Mr. New Product Head! This is Louise Smith with Doggie Delight, Inc. We are product developers and we have a brand new product that is a perfect match for your company. It is a logical extension to your line of products. And, it's patented! We are looking to license it exclusively to one manufacturer. We'd like to show it to you first.*

Mr. NPH: *You have? What is it?*

Louise: *It is a simple way to solve a problem common to dog walkers all over the world; the problem of leashes becoming entangled when walking two or more pets at the same time. It is one of those ideas that you are going to wonder why it hasn't been around before. It is so exciting and perfect for your company that we would like the opportunity to bring it and show it to you. When can we do that?*

Mr. NPH: *Just tell me what it is.*

Louise: *This product warrants a few minutes of your time. You won't be sorry if you let us come and show you. Your company needs this product. Would next week work for you? We shouldn't take up more than 20 to 30 minutes of your valuable time.*

Then, at that point, try to nail down the appointment without giving him any more specific information about your invention. We have found that when you present yourself as professional product developers and treat the manufacturers and their time with respect, they are usually more than willing to schedule an appointment to see you and your product. And, often the manufacturers don't even insist on knowing exactly what your product is if you tell them the problem that it solves. Or, you can tell them that your product is an improved (whatever). In the example above, the product is an improved pet leash.

Many Shoestring Budget™ inventors have successfully used the above-described methods to get the attention of potential licensees and actually start the negotiation process. You can do it too!

The bottom line regarding presenting your product is that you may have the greatest invention in the world, but if you are unable or unwilling to move to the next phase of product development (licensing or building a business around your invention), your invention is destined to languish in the patent books, never to reach the store shelves, as are the inventions of 97% of independent inventors in this country. This book is to help you buck those odds. Choose to be among the 3% who enjoy the thrill and satisfaction of seeing their great ideas materialized on store shelves across the country!

CHAPTER TWELVE

Licensing Agreements & Licensing Agents

Importance of Your Licensing Contract

So, you have decided to license your invention for royalties. Congratulations on having gotten this far in the process! This is an exciting time--and a nail-biting time--because you are now ready to turn your invention over to someone else. It will be out of your hands now. Or will it?

While the product will be essentially out of your hands as it relates to actually making and distributing it, you are still able to exert some control over your invention in several key areas. These areas will be included in your license agreement.

In this book, we are only discussing exclusive license agreements. Non-exclusive licensing agreements are almost entirely the domain of the very large licensors such as Disney, NASCAR, and other huge entities. These companies can license their products non-exclusively because their names are so well known that manufacturers don't mind using the same logos and images that appear on competitors' products. This is not the case with independent inventors whose products are not known. Independent inventors are licensing a brand new product, as a rule, rather than a famous image. Licensing manufacturers will demand to have exclusivity when they are taking the risk with a brand new, unknown product.

There is one exception to this situation for the independent inventor. It is possible to have more than one exclusive license agreement on the same product as long as the license agreements are in entirely separate markets. By this we mean that if your product can be used for two completely different purposes and would therefore be sold in stores that were not competing against each other for the same customers, you could license each market exclusively. This is a rare situation nowadays since the mass merchandisers often carry just about every category of product. But, if you have a product that can be sold in two totally separate markets that do not overlap, you may want to explore this possibility

When You Need to Spend Money

You have seen by now that there are many steps in developing, protecting and marketing your product that you can do for yourself and save the money that you would spend hiring someone else to do it. There are a few phases in your product development process where we advise you to spend the money on professional help if it is at all possible. You will recall that we advised you to get professional help with the writing and filing of your patent. This will be very important to you when you are ready to license your product because manufacturers will want as airtight a patent as possible. Their attorneys will look over your patent with a fine-toothed comb to be certain that they would be protected from competition if they licensed with you. They will also look it over to see if there is any way that they could circumvent your patent with one of their own and make a similar product! If they like your product well enough to consider licensing, you can be sure that they will also consider how they could get around your patent and manufacturer the product without having to license.

Once you and a manufacturer have agreed on licensing your invention, it is time to put together the actual license agreement. This is another legal document that is best left in the hands of a professional. Just as your patent can be a good strong one or a weak one, depending on the all-important wording, so the wording of your license agreement can protect your future income or cause the loss of future income for you.

In Chapter 11, we advised you to take along a sample license agreement to leave with the manufacturer when you meet with them to show your invention. This is not likely to be the agreement that you end up signing. It is only a starting point to give the manufacturer an idea of what you want. Often the manufacturer will then have his attorneys to write the agreement that they would like you to sign. You can be sure that their agreement will be totally slanted in their favor, although as someone who is unlikely to be familiar with legal language or the usual clauses in such an agreement, you might not notice all of the clauses that are to the manufacturer's definite advantage.

Even though you are watching your budget and may dislike having to pay another attorney at this point, we strongly urge you, not only to hire an attorney for this, but to hire a contract attorney. Just as your patent attorney specializes in the writing and prosecution of patents and trademarks, a contract attorney is uniquely qualified to write good, strong contracts.

Some patent attorneys are also contract attorneys. This is the best of both worlds because these attorneys are well versed in what should and should not be included in a licensing agreement for intellectual property. We know of one such attorney in the Dallas, Texas, area and we are sure that there are others around the country. You will find a link for the Dallas patent/contract attorney on the links page in the back of this book.

The manufacturer with whom you negotiate a license agreement will have a good contract attorney working for him. You will need a good attorney to protect your interests. These licensing agreements usually go back and forth between the manufacturer's and the inventor's attorney several times until every part of the agreement is hammered out to the satisfaction of all parties. It may cost you some money to have a good contract attorney, but you should look at this expense in this way: Over the long haul it won't cost you, it will pay you to have hired a contract attorney at this important junction. It could mean the difference of thousands or even hundreds of thousands of dollars in your pocket!

Below, we have included the sample license agreement that you could use to open up a licensing discussion with a manufacturer. We are not attorneys and this is only a suggested opening sample. As mentioned earlier, it is for the purpose of informing the manufacturer in general terms what you would like.

The following licensing agreement contains some of the basics of what should be included in a license agreement. You and your attorney will want to work out the clauses that will pertain to your particular situation and will specify what you expect from the licensee.

When the time comes to negotiate your licensing agreement, it is important to hire a contract attorney to help you. This expense will more than pay for itself in the long run. Many inventors rue the day they chose to forgo the help of a contract attorney. The money "saved" may be paid for dearly in the long term if your contract is not written in your best interest.

Licensing Agreement example:

March 5, 2006

LICENSING AGREEMENT

_____located at

_____

(hereinafter referred to as LICENSOR) has given

_____located at

_____

(hereinafter referred to as LICENSEE)

the exclusive production and marketing rights to
his new product concept as herein described and as
per drawings, patent applications, and/or prototype
samples previous submitted. In exchange, LICENSEE
agrees to pay LICENSOR a royalty in the amount and
under the terms outlined in this Agreement.

PRODUCT DESCRIPTION:

_____

_____

_____

1. ROYALTY PAYMENTS. A 5% (five percent) royalty, based
   on net selling price, will be paid by LICENSEE to
   LICENSOR on all sales of subject product line and
   all subsequent variations thereof by LICENSEE, its
   subsidiaries, and/or associate companies.

Page 1 of 6

The term "net selling price" shall mean the price LICENSEE receives from its customers, less any discounts for volume, promotions, defects, or freight.

Royalty payments are to be made monthly by the 30th day of the month following shipment to LICENSEE's customers, and LICENSOR shall have the right to examine LICENSEE's books and records as they pertain thereto. Further, LICENSEE agrees to reimburse LICENSOR for any legal costs he may incur in collecting overdue royalty payments. LICENSEE agrees to pay LICENSOR a guaranteed minimum royalty of $_____annually and if the agreed upon amount is not recovered by LICENSEE through sales during the annual term, such overage in royalty payments as may occur is not recoverable from future royalty years.

2. TERRITORY. LICENSEE shall have the right to market this product(s) throughout the United States, its possessions, and territories, Canada and Mexico. It may do so through any legal distribution channels it desires and in any manner it sees fit without prior approval from LICENSOR. However, LICENSEE agrees that it will not knowingly sell to parties who intend to resell the product(s) outside of the licensed territory.

3. ADVANCE PAYMENT. Upon execution of this Agreement, LICENSEE will make a nonrefundable payment to LICENSOR of $_____ which shall be construed as an advance against future earned royalties.

4. COPYRIGHT, PATENT, AND TRADEMARK NOTICES. LICENSEE agrees that on the product, its packaging and collateral material there will be printed notices of any patents issued or pending and applicable trademark and/or copyright notices showing the LICENSOR as the owner of said patents, trademarks or copyrights under exclusive license to LICENSEE.

Page 2 of 6

5. At its expense LICENSEE agrees to defend all infringement lawsuits that may be brought against it or its subsidiaries, and diligently enforce the LICENSED PATENTS and the LICENSED TRADEMARKS against all infringements brought to its attention.

In the event there has been no previous registration or patent application for the licensed product(s), LICENSEE may, at LICENSEE's discretion and expense, make such application or registration in the name of the INVENTOR. However, LICENSEE agrees that at termination or expiration of this Agreement, LICENSEE will be deemed to have assigned, transferred and conveyed to LICENSOR all trade rights, equities, goodwill, titles or other rights in and to licensed product which may have been attained by the LICENSEE. Any such transfer shall be without consideration than as specified in this Agreement.

6. TERMS AND WARRANTS. This Agreement shall be considered to be in force for so long as LICENSEE continues to sell the original product line or subsequent extensions and/or variations thereof. Further, LICENSOR agrees that, for the life of this Agreement, he will not create and/or provide directly competitive products to another manufacturer or distributor without giving the right of first refusal to LICENSEE.

7. PRODUCT DESIGNS. LICENSOR agrees to furnish conceptual product designs, if requested, for the initial product line and all subsequent variations and extensions at no charge to LICENSEE. In addition, if requested, LICENSOR will assist in the design of packaging, point-of-purchase materials, displays, etc. at no charge to LICENSEE.

However, costs for finished art, photography, typography, mechanical preparation, etc. will be borne by LICENSEE.

Page 3 of 6

Sample Licensing Agreement (continued)

8. QUALITY OF MERCHANDISE. LICENSEE agrees that Licensed product(s) will be produced and distributed in accordance with federal, state and local laws. LICENSEE further agrees to submit a sample of said product(s), its cartons, containers, and packing material to LICENSOR for approval (which approval shall not be reasonably withheld). Any item not specifically disapproved at the end of fifteen (15) working days after submission shall be deemed to be approved. The product(s) may not thereafter be materially changed without approval of the LICENSOR.

9. DEFAULT, BANKRUPTCY, VIOLATION, ETC.

   A. In the event LICENSEE does not commence to manufacture, distribute and sell product(s) within six months after the execution of this Agreement, LICENSOR, in addition to all other remedies available to him, shall have the option of canceling this Agreement. Should this event occur, to be activated by registered letter, LICENSEE agrees not to continue with the product's development and is obligated to return all prototype samples and drawings to LICENSOR.

   B. In the event LICENSEE files a petition in bankruptcy, or if the LICENSEE becomes insolvent, or makes an assignment for the benefit of creditors, the license granted hereunder shall terminate automatically without the requirement of a written notice. No further sales of licensed product(s) may be made by LICENSEE, its receivers, agents, administrators or assigns without the express written approval of the LICENSOR.

   C. If LICENSEE shall violate any other obligations under the terms of this Agreement, and upon receiving written notice of such violations by LICENSOR, LICENSEE shall have thirty (30) days to remedy such violation. If this has not been

done, LICENSOR shall have the option of canceling the Agreement upon ten (10) days written
notice. If this event occurs, all sales activity
must cease and any royalties owing are immediately due.

10. LICENSEE'S RIGHT TO TERMINATE. Notwithstanding
anything contained in this Agreement, LICENSEE
SHALL HAVE THE ABSOLUTE RIGHT TO CANCEL THIS
Agreement at any time by providing sixty (60) days
written notice to LICENSOR of his decision to discontinue the sale of the product(s) covered by
this Agreement. This cancellation shall be without
recourse from LICENSOR other than for the collection of any royalty payment that may be due him.
This notice of cancellation does not relieve
LICENSEE of responsibility for payment of any minimum royalty due for that license year.

11. INDEMNIFICATION. LICENSEE agrees to obtain, at its
own expense, product liability insurance for at
least $2,000,000 combined single unit for LICENSEE
and LICENSOR against claims, suits, loss or damage
arising out of any alleged defect in the licensed
product(s). As proof of such insurance, LICENSEE
will submit to LICENSOR a fully paid certificate of
insurance naming LICENSOR as an insured party. This
submission is to be made before any licensed product
is distributed or sold.

12. NO PARTNERSHIP, ETC. This Agreement shall be bind-
ing upon the successors and assigns of the parties
hereto. Nothing contained in this Agreement shall
be construed to place the parties in the relation-
ship of legal representatives, partners, or joint
venturers. Neither LICENSOR nor LICENSEE shall
have the power to bind or obligate in any manner
whatsoever, other than as per this Agreement.

13. GOVERNING LAW. This Agreement shall be construed
in accordance with the laws of the state of _____.

Page 5 of 6

Sample Licensing Agreement (continued)

IN WITNESS WHEREOF, the parties hereto have signed
this Agreement as of the day and year written below.

_____/_____
(LICENSEE)   (DATE)

_____/_____
(LICENSOR)   (DATE)

Having your contract worded in such a way that you are to be paid based on the net profit, rather than the net selling price can eliminate your royalty. There are ways that a company's bookkeeping can be arranged so as to never show a profit and therefore never have to pay you. *Be sure your royalty is paid on the net selling price, not net profit.*

As we previously mentioned, the above sample licensing agreement is extremely basic and not to be considered to contain some important clauses that you will need in your agreement. These are the things that a contract attorney would handle for you. For example, no mention is made of the term of the agreement as it relates to you. You should be able to renew the agreement at specific intervals, every two to four years, in order to renegotiate terms or to discontinue the agreement if you wish. Also, your right to audit the records of your licensee should be clearly defined regarding what can be audited and at what intervals. These and other important details are good reasons for having the best contract attorney you can get for writing and negotiating the terms of your agreement.

Legitimate Licensing Agents

In Chapter 11, we discussed how to create a great presentation and make the appointment with the manufacturer for a licensing discussion. If you absolutely cannot present your own product because you are paralyzed with fear or you simply do not have the time or the confidence to do it, the next best thing is to hire a legitimate licensing agent to do it for you.

 Find legitimate licensing agents from personal referrals, trusted sources such as the:
- **United Inventors' Association** *at* www.uiausa.org
- **Inventors' Digest Magazine** *at* www.inventorsdigest.com
- **Ask the Inventors!** *at* www.asktheinventors.com
  or your local inventors' club or association.

Not every sector of the market is represented by legitimate licensing agents. If your invention falls into one of the "agent-poor" sectors of the market, it may require some work and creativity on your part to identify and locate someone to represent your product to potential licensees. The most direct route to finding a legitimate agent who can accomplish the task for you is to identify your potential licensee and simply call them. Ask them if they work with licensing agents. If they do, ask for the names and contact information of the agents with whom they have worked before. If they work with licensing agents, they will usually provide this information to you. At that point, you simply contact the agent and ask him if he would be interested in representing your product.

If you cannot get the name of a licensing agent with whom your licensing targets currently work, you can choose a nonspecific licensing agent who is willing to work in virtually any sector of the market. These agents are extremely selective about the products they will represent. It may be more difficult to get one of them to sign on to your product if it is an area of the market in which they have little or no experience. But if they are overwhelmed with the brilliance and market potential of your product, they may be willing to do so. Before agreeing to entrust them with the marketing of your product, check out their licensing track record. Ask them for references.

There is an international organization of licensing executives with chapters in every state. This organization is made up of individuals who are involved in licensing in all areas. Some of them are attorneys, others are licensing agents who are not attorneys and some are ancillary people who have some connection with licensing such as consultants, engineers, scientists, etc. This organization is the **Licensing Executives Society** and their stated purpose on their website is, "(LES) is a professional society comprised of over 6,000 members engaged in the transfer, use, development, manufacture and marketing of intellectual property." You can access their website for the United States and Canada at: http://www.usa-canada.les. org/. The fact that they are members of this society does not necessarily reflect their abilities, reputations, or their records of accomplishment. As always, ask for references and check them out for yourself.

Licensing agents charge a fee, usually in the form of a share of the royalty percentage they negotiate on your behalf. Typically, the agreement between you and the licensing agents is set up so that the royalties are sent to the agent who deposits the check, and then writes you a check for the remainder after his percentage has been deducted. Fees for legitimate licensing agents can be fairly steep. It is not unusual for a licensing agent to take 40-60% of the royalty in exchange for his services. Sometimes it is a lesser percentage for the lifetime of the product and sometimes it is a larger percentage for a shorter time period. Some agent percentages are on a sliding scale, depending on the amount of royalty involved. If they are very good at what they do and they agree to represent your product, your work is over at this point. While it may cost you in terms of your future royalties, if you are absolutely not able to represent yourself for whatever reason, this may be the best route for you. A share of something, is always better than all of nothing. That is the way you need to think of it if the alternative is untenable to you.

CHAPTER THIRTEEN

Toys
Shoestring Inventing At Its Best!

Patents on Toys

For the Shoestring Budget™ inventor's first foray into the world of inventing, selecting a toy idea can be the least expensive route to success. Lest you incorrectly assume that toy inventing is easy, let us disabuse you of that notion right off. Toy inventing is not easy, but it can be the least costly type of invention to pursue.

Let us explain . . . the toy industry is a very specialized sector of the market and this sector does not follow the same product introduction rules that are followed by the rest of the market. The toy market is a multibillion-dollar international industry and it is extremely fast moving. By that, we mean that from idea to market is often a much shorter time in the toy industry than it is for other categories of inventions.

The reason for this circumstance is that, unlike other types of products that may enjoy years of shelf life in basically the same form, toys are ever changing in response to the constant consumer demand for new items. Unless a toy has a continuing high level of sales, it is replaced within a season or two by new toys. Because of this situation, the toy industry simply

153

does not have the time to wait for patents. If manufacturers waited to receive a patent on each toy before introducing it into the market, their competitors would bury them. Trends would come and go while the toy company was still waiting on the excruciatingly slow patent office to process its patent applications. Because of this, most toys are not even patented.

There are exceptions, of course. Lasting toys that corner a specific sector of the toy market are sometimes patented. The Barbie® Doll and Hot Wheels® cars are examples of toys that would appropriately be protected by patents. Most beginning toy inventors do not have the next Barbie® or the next Hot Wheels®, so for those novice toy inventors, a patent would not be required or even desired. The absence of patent-related expenses for most toy inventions is the first big savings for the Shoestring Budget™ inventor. The patent is usually the most expensive part of the entire inventive process and in toy inventing it can be omitted in most cases.

For the beginning toy inventor who does have the next Barbie® or Hot Wheels®, the news is good, too. Once the manufacturer has selected your toy idea to pursue, if it is determined that a patent would be advantageous, they would at least share the patenting costs if they did not pay for the patent expenses entirely. If the toy manufacturer did choose to file for patent protection on your toy idea, you would be listed as the inventor and the patent would belong to you even though the toy company initiated all the work on the patent and paid the costs of obtaining it.

Toy Prototypes

Prototyping of toys is different from prototyping inventions for the general market. The way that you approach prototyping will be determined by the way you wish to market the toy. Toy developers normally choose between three courses of action. As a toy inventor, you may elect to go through a toy agent if you hope to have your toy picked up by one of the major toy companies. You may choose to go directly to one of the smaller specialty toy companies for placement of your toy with them, or you may become your own manufacturer and take your toy to one or more of the large shows such as Toy Fair in New York. The approach to prototyping your toy or game is different for each of these courses of action.

Toy Agents

If you, as the inventor of a toy, want to pursue one of the big toy companies, you would be wise to use a toy agent. The large toy manufacturers simply do not have the time or the inclination to meet with independent toy developers. They prefer instead to work with a few toy agents who bring them multiple toys and who are accustomed to presenting them in a short amount of time.

Toy executives have a keen sense of what works or does not work for their company and they can generally make a 'gut assessment' in a matter of minutes of whether they would be interested in pursuing any particular toy. If you choose to pursue this course of action, your job is to convince the toy agent that you have the type of toy that he could successfully represent to that company.

So, what kind of toys are agents seeking? Toy agents are looking for safe toys that are fun to play with! They want toys in which the goal of the play is easy to understand, toys that do not require a lot of instruction, and they want toys that will encourage repeated use.

A toy agent will assess your idea based on its concept. He generally does not require a prototype of your toy at the time of your initial submission to him. If he likes your idea, the agent may request a working prototype. If you have a working prototype, you can send it along at that point. If you do not have a working prototype, the toy agent can work with you to have a prototype made.

Find a toy agent by calling the company with which you wish to place your toy. Ask to speak to their inventor liaison. If they do not have a position with this particular title, they will know who should receive your call. When you get them on the phone, ask them for the name and contact information for the toy agents with whom they prefer to work. They will be happy to provide you with that information. At that point, give the agent a call and request his submission process.

Toy agents do a great deal of the work involved in getting your toy to market. In addition to helping with the prototyping if necessary, the toy agent also will present your toy to the big toy companies and probably even cover the legal costs associated with negotiating a license agreement for you. Toy agents do a lot of the work for you and they often charge hefty fees in return.

It is not unusual for a toy agent to charge a nominal fee to even look at your idea as well as sharing 50-60 percent of your royalty if he is able to obtain a license agreement. The reason for this submission charge is that a legitimate toy agent has to do much more than just look at the toy to determine if it is a marketing possibility. He has to do a great deal of research. Since many toys are not patented, these agents maintain large libraries of toy catalogs from all over the world, which they must search. This is in addition to searching the patent database to make sure that your toy idea does not infringe upon an existing patent. We made the statement earlier that patents are generally not required for toys, and this is true. But, many inventors do choose to file for patents on their toy inventions, making it necessary to conduct a patent search before proceeding with development and/or licensing of toy ideas.

Though their prices are steep, toy agents do have the eyes and ears of the toy executives that you, as an independent toy developer, do not have. It is often well worth the cost if you are able to get your toy licensed by one of the big toy manufacturers. The wide national or even international distribution of your toy by one of the big manufacturers can be very lucrative and can more than make up for sharing the royalty with the toy agent.

Small Specialty Toy Companies

Though these companies are not the names that immediately pop into mind when you think of toy companies, don't let the fact that they are called "small" fool you. Small specialty toy companies often have wide distribution. Small specialty toy companies are unique in that they specialize in a particular sector of the toy market. For example, Atomic Toys specializes in toys for boys ages 8-18. Atomic Toys manufactures several sports board games as well as remote controlled vehicles of various kinds from cars to airplanes. Within that particular market, Atomic Toys does very well. They have national and international distribution of their products and they have been recognized within the toy industry as an up and coming company.

There are many, many specialty toy companies, each directing its efforts toward a specific sector of the toy market. You may be able to locate the specialty toy company that would be interested in your invention idea by simply looking on the labels of toys that fall into the same general category.

Independent toy developers do not need a toy agent to represent them to these smaller toy companies. You, the independent toy inventor, can do that yourself and save a bundle in the process since any license agreement you and your attorney negotiate will not have to be shared with a toy agent. These smaller companies often welcome submissions from independent toy designers.

You will need a prototype to present to the specialty toy manufacturers, but your toy prototype does not need to be shelf ready. We mean by this that your prototype does not have to look exactly as it will look on the store shelves. In this prototype stage it needs only to be a working model to show how it works and that it does work. Obviously, the better your toy prototype looks, the easier it will be for the toy manufacturers to visualize it as a part of their toy line. So, make the best prototype you can, but don't be a perfectionist. Do everything to make your prototype look as good as possible without spending a lot of money.

For example, if your product is a board game with cards used for play, laminate the cards yourself. You can do this using clear Contact paper (available at most grocery stores) rather than taking it to a Kinko's type store and paying for professional laminating service. By using your creativity and ingenuity, you can prepare a good-looking prototype without breaking the bank. If you find a toy manufacturer that agrees to license your toy idea, that manufacturer will get it produced and packaged.

 If your toy or game requires a plastic prototype, you can make a great looking one yourself with Randall Landreneau's guide, **How to Make Plastic Prototypes** at:

www.plasticprototypes.net

Randall's video guide leads you through how to make a great looking, but inexpensive plastic prototype with materials that are readily available. There is a coupon for a 15% discount off this video in the coupon section at the back of this book. If you prefer to have your plastic prototype made, rather than doing it yourself, you can get a reasonably priced great looking plastic prototype using rapid prototyping services. (Described more fully in Chapter 6, Prototyping)

If you choose to approach the smaller toy companies with your toy you are, in effect, acting as your own agent and saving yourself the cost of hiring an agent. When you act as your own agent, you have to do the work an agent would normally perform. You have been creative enough to come up with a great toy idea, right? There is no reason why you cannot be creative enough to come up with a compelling presentation for your toy invention in addition to the prototype.

In your presentation, you need to explain why your toy fits into their toy line and how it might expand their market share. If you have documentation of consumer acceptance, (i.e. focus group studies showing children's response to your toy or game) include that also. Letters from test users about how much they liked the toy or game, how easy and how much fun it was to play will be helpful. Do not make statements like, "All the kids in my neighborhood played with my toy and they said it was the best toy they ever played with!" or "My kids and my nieces and nephews love my toy!" Those types of statements may cause them to discount your entire presentation and even your toy. Toy manufacturers consider such statements amateurish.

If a small specialty toy company agrees to license your product, have any license agreement examined and approved by your attorney. A contract attorney is best. If you do not know one, you can find one through your local inventor club or by contacting the **Licensing Executives Society** at:

`www.usa-canada.les.org`

Toy Associations and Shows

Some independent toy developers have chosen to build a business around their toys. If you choose to follow their example then you would become your own manufacturer. In many cases, you will find that by having your toy manufactured offshore you will be able to do it at a fraction of the cost of domestic manufacturing. Obviously, when you become your own manufacturer, the prototyping process is simply to get the toy in its final form to your own satisfaction. You are the only one you are trying to please at this point, other than the eventual end user.

When, as a toy or game designer, you choose to become the manufacturer, your most daunting task will be to get your toy on the shelves of the retail stores. Other independent toy designers who have chosen this path have overcome this obstacle by joining the professional toy associations and taking their toys to one or more of the major toy shows (find a listing of major toy shows in the appendix at the back of this book). The buyers for all of the retail stores that carry toys attend the toy shows and if they like your toy, they may place an order for their store. The samples you have on display at a toy show must be the final product. Prototypes will not do. Retail buyers want to see the toy exactly as it will appear on their store shelves.

If you choose to start your own toy company featuring your toy, we recommend that you join one or more of the trade associations of the toy industry such as:

The Toy Industry Association at:

`www.toy-tia.org`

Women in Toys Association at:

`www.womenintoys.com/profile_PattyBecker.html`

or **American Specialty Toys Retail Association** at:

`www.astratoy.org/i4a/pages/index.cfm?pageid=1`

This is essential if you are to be taken seriously within the industry. It is also a good idea to subscribe to the toy industry trade magazines such as **Playthings Magazine** at:

`www.playthings.com`

or **Games Quarterly** at:

`www.gamesquarterly.net`

The Toy Industry Association's annual Toy Fair occurs each February in New York and it is probably the largest of the toy shows. As a toy manufacturer, you will be entitled to register not only to attend but also to have a booth featuring your toy. Booth rates depend upon the size and location. Rates are based on a per square foot charge. For example, at the 2006 Toy Fair, booths cost $26 per square foot for non-members of the association and $20 per square foot for members with an additional $200 for a corner booth. Although this may sound a little steep for a Shoestring Budget™ toy developer, if you are choosing to be the manufacturer of your toy it will give you your best chance at getting your product picked up by all the stores that sell toys. Another way to look at this expense is to determine how much product you would have to sell in order to pay that booth rental and your other expenses related to being there (transportation, hotel, etc.). After you have sold that amount of product, it is all profit. Additionally, look at all of the visibility you have gotten for your toy that could result in future sales.

The second major toy show where you should consider attending and displaying your product is the **Toys n Games Show, TGIF** at:

www.toysngames.com/tgif/tgifover.htm

This is the show that was formerly presented each year in Las Vegas. For the past few years, it has been held in Orlando. TGIF consists of a conference and exhibition.

The associations as well as the trade magazines will help you to stay on top of the trends. Participation in the associations and careful reading of the magazines and journals will also familiarize you with the major players and happenings within the industry. With the right toy and the right initiatives, you could one day be one of those major players!

Shoestring Budget™ toy developers/manufacturers who cannot afford to rent a booth in which to display their toys or games can still benefit from going to the shows. You will not get the exposure for your toy that you would get from having a booth, but you can meet many of the retailers who carry toys and other toy manufacturers simply by attending and mingling. If you have been studying the association newsletters and trade magazines, you may have learned the names of key players in the toy industry. Those people will be at the toy shows. Keep your eyes on the name tags. When you see a name you recognize, walk up and introduce yourself. In this way you will begin to network and be recognized as a member of the "club" also known as toy industry insiders.

There are two ways you can benefit from attending the shows even if you do not set up a booth. First, as you walk the show you will see all the retailers who carry toys in their stores. This will allow you to identify every possible outlet for your toy. After the show, when you contact those toy manufacturers and introduce yourself as having been at the show they will accept that you are an industry insider (Why else would you have been at the show?). Second, you will meet all the other toy manufacturers. You may happen upon a manufacturer who would love to license your toy! If that is the case, you will be in the happy position of deciding whether you wish to continue manufacturing and distributing your toy on your own, or handing it off to an established manufacturer that already has the distribution channels and shelf space allotted in the stores.

One additional benefit of attending a toy show as a spectator is that you will have an opportunity to see the trends of the toy industry. Toy manufacturers have their fingers on the pulse of what types of toys will be popular in coming seasons. You will see the direction of these trends in the toys that are displayed, an important advantage whether you wish to license or to continue developing new toys.

 Do not try to approach retailers or manufacturers on the first days of the show when they are selling their products to their retail customers. Wait until the last day when the retailers are just waiting to close up. At that time, the people manning the booths will be happy to visit with you and perhaps even take a look at your toy.

Whatever course of action you choose to pursue with your toy, you can see that toy inventing offers the many benefits of regular inventing; creativity, joy of seeing your product on the market and a stream of income created by your toy, with few of the expenses. Toy and game inventing truly is Shoestring Budget™ inventing at its best.

Summary of Steps

This summary is intended merely as a general guideline that we personally recommend. It is not a hard and fast rule that the steps must be taken in exactly this order. The order of some steps may be reversed or entire steps may be eliminated altogether at your discretion. This is provided as a checklist to help you to be certain that you are continuously moving forward with your product.

1. Idea
2. Inventor's journal
3. Disclosure Document
4. Market search
5. Preliminary patent search
6. Prototype
7. Professional patent search
8. Professional product evaluation
9. Refine prototype
10. File for patent protection
11. Decide whether to license or build a business around your invention

If you choose licensing:

1. Identify potential licensees or hire a licensing agent
2. Prepare written product presentation
3. Prepare oral product presentation
4. Make the calls to make the appointment with potential licensees
5. Meet with manufacturers to present your product
6. Engage contract attorney to help negotiate your license agreement

If you choose to create a business around your invention:

1. Make a business plan and implement
2. Arrange for manufacturing, packaging and distribution
3. Market your invention to retailers

Conclusion

While Shoestring Budget™ inventing may not be the fastest or the easiest way to get your idea to market, it is definitely the smartest way if you do not have a substantial amount of money set aside with which to pursue your invention idea. Even the greatest of ideas will face hurdles in getting to market. The risk of failure is very high in independent inventing. Independent inventors/product developers must accept the reality of this situation. Shoestring Budget™ inventing allows the independent inventor to limit his cash outlay on any one idea and preserve resources for future invention ideas. Shoestring Budget™ inventors, like all inventors, are a very creative group and they almost always have multiple ideas for many inventions. We sincerely hope that the idea you are now pursuing is THE IDEA that will bring you success and financial security. However, if it is not, Shoestring Budget™ inventing will allow you to go after your dream without depleting your savings and preventing you from being able to pursue another of your ideas that could succeed in the marketplace.

Shoestring Budget™ inventing requires patience, perseverance, creativity and determination. If you possess these qualities, your chances of getting your great idea to market are greatly enhanced. Keep your goal in mind, set aside the time required to keep moving forward and don't take no for an answer! If you encounter obstacles along the way, and you can be certain that you will, do not simply accept them. Engage your creativity and find another way to keep moving forward.

Here's to you, a Shoestring Budget™ inventor on your way to success! If you need a helping hand along the way, refer to our website, *Ask the Inventors!* We will be posting more money-saving ideas and opportunities there as we learn of them. If you have learned of a way to save money during the inventive journey we would love to hear about it. Please write to us and tell us your ways of saving money and we may include them in the next edition of this book.

Follow your dream!

Mary & Barb

mary@asktheinventors.com
barb@asktheinventors.com

Appendix A
Inventors Clubs

National Organizations

National Congress of Inventor Organizations
Stephen Gnass
PO Box 931881
Los Angeles, CA 90093
Phone: (323) 878-6952
E-mail: ncio@inventionconvention.com/ncio

United Inventors Association of the USA
Carol Oldenburg
PO Box 23447
Rochester, NY 14692
Phone: (585) 359-9310
E-mail: UIAUSA@aol.com
Website: www.uiausa.org

International Organizations

International Federation of Inventors' Associations (IFIA)
A non-governmental organization created by inventor associations in 1968.
The organization consists of members from 100 countries.
Website: http://www.invention-ifia.ch

The Inventors Association of Australia
Website: www.inventors.asn.au

Association of Hungarian Inventors (MAFE)
Vedres Andras
Phone: +3620 945 8078
Website: www.inventor.hu

New Zealand Inventors
Ian Montanjees
E-mail: imontanjees@xtra.co.nz

Wellington Inventors Group
John Poppleton
Wellington, New Zealand
E-mail: j_poppleton@paradise.net.nz
Website: www.kiwiingenuity.net

Wessex Round Table of Inventors
Mike Overy
Southampton, Hampshire (UK)
Website: www.wrti.org.UK

Hamad Al-Ba'adi
King Abdulaziz' Foundation for Gifted
PO Box 300820
Riyadh, Alriyadh, Saudi Arabia
Phone: 9-661-462-9462
E-mail: info@gifted.org.sa

Canada

Inventors Alliance of Canada
Mark Ellwood
350 Sunnyside Ave.
Toronto, Ontario M6R 2R6
Phone: (416) 410-7792
E-mail: ellwood@netcom.ca
Website: www.inventorsalliance.com

British Columbia Inventors' Society
Richard Parson
PO Box 78055
Vancouver, BC V5N 5W1
Phone: Joann Robertson (604) 707-0250 or (604) 838-9185
E-mail: admin@bcinventor.com
Website: www.bcinventor.com

Durham East Independent Inventors' Group
Pickering, Ontario
Phone: (905) 686-7172
E-mail: gc7591@hotmail.com

Inter Atlantic Inventors Club
Tomas Romero
28021 Tacoma PO
Dartmouth, NS B2W 6E2
Phone: (902) 435-5218

Inventors Club of Brantford
Les Sutch
73 Palace Street,
Brantford, Ontario N3T 3W8
Phone: (519) 753-7735
E-mail: G.Schram: grahamschram@hotmail.com

Saskatchewan Research Council
Marie Savostianik
15 Innovation Blvd.
Saskatoon, Saskatchewan S7N 2X8
Phone: (306) 933-5400

Women's Inventor's Project – Toronto, Canada
107 Holm Crescent
Thornhill, Ontario L3T 5J4
Phone: (905) 731-9691
Website: www.interlog.com/~womenip

Waterloo-Wellington Inventors Club
Cambridge, Ontario
Phone: (519) 653-8848
E-mail: svandyk@bserv.com

Alabama

Alabama Inventors Club
Francisco Guerra c/o Snowmasters
3481 County Road 93
Anderson, AL 35610
Phone: (256) 229-5551
E-mail: Francisco@snowmasters.com
Mike Hubka
Phone: (256) 331-5270
E-mail: hubka@nwscc.edu

Invent Alabama
Bruce Koppenhoefer
137 Mission Circle
Montevallo, AL 35115
Phone: (866) 745-6319 or (205) 663-9982
E-mail: bkoppy@hiwaay.net or BKOPPENHOE@aol.com

Alaska

Alaska Inventors & Entrepreneurs
Pam Middaugh
PO Box 241801
Anchorage, AK 99524-1801
Phone: (907) 563-4337
E-mail: inventor@artic.net
Website: www.artic.net/~inventor

Inventors Institute of Alaska
Al Jorgensen
PO Box 876154
Wasilla, AK 99687
Phone: (907) 376-5114

Arizona

Arizona Inventors Association
Valerie Becket, Executive Director
PO Box 6436
Glendale, AZ 85312
Phone: (800) 299-6787 (Phoenix)
E-mail: vbecket@azdot.gov
Website: www.azinventors.org

Arkansas

Inventors Congress, Inc.
Garland Bull
Rt 2, Box 1630
Dardanell, AR 72834
Phone: (501) 229-4515

California

Inventors Forum
Mike Falley
PO Box 8008
Huntington Beach, CA 92615
Phone: (714) 540-2491 or (562)464-0069
Website: www.inventorsforum.org

Inventors Alliance
Andrew Krauss, President
PO BOX 390219
Mountain View, CA 94039
Phone: 650-964-1576
E-mail: president7@InventorsAlliance.org or andrewinvents@onebox. com
Website: www.inventorsalliance.org/index.cgi?internet

Inventors Alliance
(Live Internet Chapter Meetings)
Andrew Krauss
PO Box 390219
Mountain View, CA
94039-390219
Phone: (650) 964-1576
Email: president7@InventorsAlliance.org
Website: www.inventorsalliance.org/index.cgi?internet

InventNET Forum
10531 Royal Oak Way
Stanton, CA 90680
E-mail: info@inventnet.com

Inventors Alliance – Sacramento
Ed Silva
Phone: (906) 224-9076
Website: www.inventorsalliance.org

Contra Costa Inventors Club
Sherm Fishman
295 Stevenson Drive
Pleasant Hill, CA 94523-4149
Phone: (510) 934-1331

Inventors Forum of San Diego
Greg Lauren
11292 Poblado Road
San Diego, CA 92127
Phone: (858) 451-1028 or (619) 673-4733
E-mail: Enovex@aol.com

Bruce Sawyer Center
Steve Schneider or Charles Robbins
4261 Brookshire Circle
Santa Rosa, CA 95405
Phone: (707) 524-1773
E-mail: sbdc1@ap.net

American Inventor Network
Jeff McGrew
1320 High School Rd.
Sebastopol, CA 95472
Phone: (707) 823-3865

Inventors Alliance of Northern California
Jim DeLang
6514 Elmira Drive
Redding, CA 96001
Phone: (530) 241-5222 or (530) 241-8427
E-mail: sagn@charter.net
Website: www.inventorsnorcal.org

Idea to Market Network
Sidnee Cox
PO Box 12248, Santa Rosa, CA 95406
Phone: 1-800-ITM-3210
E-mail: sidnee@ap.net
Website: www.ideatomarket.org

Colorado

Rocky Mountain Inventors Congress
1852 S. Cole St.
Lakewood, CO 80228
Phone: (303) 670-3760(answering service)
E-mail: RMInventor@yahoo.com
Website: www.RMInventor.org

Connecticut

Christian Inventors Association
Pal Asija
7 Woonsocket Ave.
Shelton, CT 06484
Phone: (203) 924-9538
E-mail: pal@ourpal.com

Danbury Innovators Guild
Danbury, CT
Phone: (203) 426-4205
E-mail: iambest2@juno.com

Innovators Guild
Robin Faulkner
2 Worden Road
Danbury, CT 06811
Phone:(203) 790-8235
E-mail: RFaulkner@snet.net

Inventors Assn. of Connecticut
Bob Distinti, Vice President
46 Rutland Ave.
Fairfield, CT 06825
Phone: (203) 331-9696 or (203) 866-0720
E-mail: IACT@inventus.org (John Ruhnke, Pres.)
Website: www.inventus.org

Delaware

Early Stage East
3 Mill Road, Ste 201A
Wilmington, DE 19806
Phone: (302) 777-2460
E-mail: info@earlystageeast.org

Delaware Entrepreneurs Forum
Colleen Wolf
PO Box 278
Yorklyn, DE 19736
Phone: (302) 652-4241

District of Columbia

Inventors Network of the Capital Area
Ray Gilbert
6501 Inwood Drive
Springfield, VA 22150
Phone: (703) 971-7443 or (703) 971-9216
E-mail: Raybik@aol.com or info@inca.hispeed.net
Website: www.dcinventors.org

Florida

Inventors Soc. of South Florida
John Fulton
Malloy & Malloy, P.A.
2800 SW Third Avenue
Miami, FL 33129
PO Box 4306
Boynton Beach, FL 33424
Phone: (800) 337-7239 or (954) 486-2426
E-mail: jfulton@malloylaw.com
Website: www.InventorsSociety.net

Edison Inventors Association, Inc.
Gary Nelson
Box 07398
Ft. Myers, FL 33919
Phone: (941) 267-9746 or (941) 275-4332
E-mail: drghn@aol.com
Website: www.edisoninventors.org

Emerald Coast Inventors' Society
Earnie DeVille
C/O UWF-SBDC
11000 University
Pensacola, FL 32514-5752
Phone: (904) 455-4641

Tampa Bay Inventors' Council
Jennifer Knoepp
7441 114th Avenue North, Suite 607
Largo, FL 33773-5124
Phone: (727) 548-5083 or (727) 866-0669
E-mail: KIEWIT@patent-faq.com
Website: patent-faq.com/tbichome.htm

Inventors Council of Central Florida
David Flinchbaugh
4855 Big Oaks Lane
Orlando, FL 32806-7826
Phone: (407) 859-4855
E-mail: david@urosolutions.com

Palm Isles Inventors Group
A. Morton Rosenfield, Pres.
9528 Shadybrook Dr, Ste 102
Boynton Beach, FL 33437-6138
Phone: (561) 739-9259 or 9439

Space Coast Inventors Guild
Angel L. Pacheco, Sr.
1221 Pine Tree Dr.
Indian Harbour Beach, FL 32937
Phone: (321) 773-4031

Tampa Bay Inventors Council
Jennifer Knoepp
7441 114th Avenue North, Ste 606
Largo, FL 33773-5124
Phone: (727) 548-5083 or (727) 866-0669
E-mail: jennifer@tbic.us
Website: www.tbic.us

Georgia

Inventor Assoc. of Georgia, Inc.
Ron Reardon or Bob Miquelon
1608 Pelham Way
Macon, GA 31220
Phone: (770) 241-4907 or (912) 474-6948
E-mail: rreardon@bellsouth.net
Website: www.geocities.com/iaggroup

Hawaii

Hawaii-International Inventors Association, Inc.
Richard Sakoda
945 Makaiwa Street
Honolulu, HI 96816
Phone: (808) 523-5555
E-mail: sakodaesq@aol.com

Idaho

East Idaho Inventors Forum
John Wordin
PO Box 452
Shelly, ID
Phone: (208) 346-6763
E-mail: wordinjj@ida.net or techhelp@srv.net

Illinois

Inventors' Council
Don Moyer
431 South Dearborne #705
Chicago, IL 60605
Phone: (312) 939-3329
E-mail: patent@donmoyer.com
Website: www.donmoyer.com

Illinois Innovators & Inventor's Club
Phil Curry
PO Box 623
Edwardsville, IL 62025
Phone: (618) 656-7445
E-mail: Invent@Charter-IL.com

Illinois Group
Dr. Tom Honsa
3637 23rd Avenue
Moline, Il 61265
Phone: (309) 762-6936

Indiana

Indiana Inventors Association
Robert Humbert
5514 South Adams
Marion, IN 46953
Phone: (765) 674-2845
E-mail: arhumbert@bpsinet.com

Iowa

Drake University Inventure Program
Ben Swartz
SBDC-Drake University
2507 University Avenue
Des Moines, IA 50311
Phone: (515) 271-2655

Kansas

Inventors Association of south Central Kansas
Richard Freidenberger
2302 North Amarado Street
Wichita, KS, 67205
Phone: (316) 721-1866
E-mail: Richard@inventkansas.com
Website: www.inventkansas.com

Kansas Association of Inventors
Clayton Williamson
272 W. 6th St.
Hoisington, KS 67544
Phone: (316) 653-2165
E-mail: clayton@hoisington.com

Mid-America Inventors Association
David Herron
PO Box 2778
Kansas City, KS 66110
Phone: (913) 371-7011
E-mail: midamerica-inventors@kc.rr.com
Website: www.midamerica-inventors.com

Kentucky

Central Kentucky Inventors Council, Inc.
Donald L. West, President
3060 Pine Ridge Road
Winchester, KY 40391
Phone: (859) 842-4110 or (606) 885-9593
E-mail: dlwest3@yahoo.com

Louisiana

Louisiana Inventors Association
14724 Vinewood Drive
Baton Rouge, LA 70816
Phone: (225) 752-3783
E-mail: info@recyclecycle.com

Maine

Portland Inventors Forum--
Dept Industrial Co-op
Jake Ward
University of Maine
5717 Corbett Hall
Orono, ME 04469-5717
Phone: (207)581-1488
E-mail: jsward@maine.edu
Website: www.umaine.edu/DIC

Maryland/District of Columbia

(See listing under District of Columbia)

Massachusetts

Cape Cod Inventors Association
Ernest Bauer
Briar Main -- PO Box 143
Wellfleet, MA 02667
Phone: (508) 349-1628 or (508) 349-1629
E-mail: cdwbauer@msn.com

Greater Boston Inventors Association
Inventors Association of New England
Chris Holt
PO Box 577
Pepperal, MA 01463
Phone: (978) 433-2397
E-mail: crholt@aol.com
Website: www.inventne.org

Innovators Resource Network
(Please note that group meets in Springfield, MA)
Dave Cormier and Karyl Lynch
Pelham West Associates
PO Box 137
Shutesbury, MA 01072-0137
Phone: (413) 259-2006
E-mail: info@IRNetwork.org
Website: www.IRNetwork.org

Worcester Area Inventors
Jeff White
25 Warren Street
Upton, MA 01568
Phone: (508) 529-3552 – (508) 791-0226 – (508) 835-6435
E-mail: swcei@aol.com or Barbara@nedcorp.com

Michigan

Inventors Association of Metropolitan Detroit
Frank Wales
749 Clairepointe Circle
St. Claire, MI 48081
Phone: (810) 772-7888
E-mail: unclefj@yahoo.com

Inventors' Council of Mid-Michigan
Tim Langan, President
E-mail: Cliotech@chartermi.net
Ron Brogquist, Membership Director
E-mail: ICEI@webtv.net or lford22649@aol.com
11403 Bray Road
Clio, MI 48420
Phone: (810) 516-8564or (810) 232-7909 or (810) 233-7437
Website: www.flintchamber.org or www.rjriley.com/icmm

InventorEd, Inc.
Ronald J Riley
1323 West Cook Road
Grand Blanc, MI 48439
E-mail: rjriley@InventorEd.org
Phone: (810) 655-8830
Website: www.rjriley.com/icmm or www.inventored.org

The Enterpreneur Network
Ed Zimmer
350 Corrie Road
Ann Arbor, MI 48105
Phone: (800) 468-8871
E-mail: edzimmer@tenonline.org

Minnesota

Society of Minnesota Inventors
Paul Paris
13055 Riverdale Drive
Suite 500
Coon Rapids, MN
Phone: (763) 753-2766 or (612) 753-2766
E-mail: PGPENT@yahoo.com

Inventors' Network (Minneapolis./St Paul)
Bill Baker
23 Empire Dr., Ste. 105
St. Paul, MN 55103
Phone: (651) 602-3175 or (651) 374-5234
Website: www.inventorsnetwork.org

Minnesota Inventors Congress
Jennifer Moritz, Coordinator
PO Box 71
Redwood Falls, MN 56283-0071
Phone: (507) 637-2344 or 1-800-468-3681
E-mail: mic@invent1.org
Website: www.invent1.org

Mississippi

Mississippi SBDC Inventor Assistance
Bob Lantrip
B 19 Jeanette Phillips Dr.
University, MS 38677
Phone: (662) 915-5001 or (601) 232-5001 or(800) 725-7232 (MS only)
E-mail: blantrip@olemiss.edu
Website: www.olemiss.edu/depts/mssbdc/invent.html

Society of Mississippi Inventors
Michele Davis
1923 Spillway Rd., #221
Brandon, MS 39047
Phone: (601) 238-2402
E-mail: gwe2121@bellsouth.net
Website: www.msinventors.org

Missouri

Center for Business & Economic Development
Dr. Gerald Udell,Univ.of SW Missouri State
901 S National Ave.
Springfield, MO 65804
Phone: (417) 836-5671
E-mail: geraldudell@smsu.edu

Mid-America Inventors Association
Carl Minzes
8911 East 29th St.
Kansas City, MO 64129-1502
Phone: (816) 254-9542

Inventors Association of St. Louis
Robert Scheinkman
PO Box 410111
St. Louis, MO 63141
Phone: (314) 432-1291
Website: www.communityconnection.org/resource_pages/42646.html

Women Inventors Project
Betty Rozier
7400 Foxmount
Hazlewood, MO 63042
Phone: (314) 432-1291

Montana

Blue Sky Inventors
Warren George
1200 Blair Lane, Apt. #1
Billings, MT 59102
Phone: (406) 259-9110 or (406) 586-1541

Montana Inventors Association.
Casey Emerson
5350 Love Lane
Bozeman, MT 59715
Phone: (406) 586-1541

Yellowstone Inventors
Warren George
3 Carrie Lynn
Billings, MT 59102
Phone: (406) 259-9110

Nebraska

Lincoln Inventors Association
Roger Reyda
92 Ideal Way
Brainard, NE 68626
Phone: (402) 545-2179 Fax: Same
Website: assist.ded.state.ne.us/invent.html

Nevada

Nevada Inventors Association
Vince Chemist
PO Box 11008
Reno, NV 89510-1108
Phone: (775) 677-0123 or (775) 677-4824
E-mail: infor@nevadainventors.org
Website: www.nevadainventors.org

Inventors Society of Southern Nevada
Penny J. Ballou
3627 Huerta Drive
Las Vegas, NV 89121
Phone: (702) 435-7741
E-mail: InventSSN@aol.com

New Hampshire

New Hampshire Inventors Association
John Rocheleau
PO Box 272
Concord, NH 03202
Phone: (603) 228-3854
E-mail: john@nhinventor.com

New Jersey

Jersey Shore Inventors Club
 Bill Hincher
23 Pittenger Pond Rd.
Freehold, NJ 07728
Phone: (732) 407-8885 or (732) 776-8467 or (732) 776-8467

Kean Univ. SBDC
Mira Kostak
215 North Ave. - rm 242
Union, NJ 07083
Phone: (908) 737-5950 or (908) 527-2946

National Society of Inventors
Shelia Kalisher
94 North Rockledge Dr.
Livingston, NJ 07039-1121
Phone: (973) 994-9282
Website: www.NationalInventors.com

New Jersey Entrepreneurs Forum
Jeff Milanette
PO Box 313
Westfield, NJ 07091-3424
Phone: (908) 789-3424
E-mail: JMilanette@aol.com
Website: www.njef.org

New Mexico

New Mexico Inventors Club
Albert Goodman
PO Box 30062
Albuquerque, NM 87190
Phone: (505) 266-3541

New York

The Aurora Club
Richard Guard
11880 Centerline Road
South Wales, NY 14139 (located South East of Buffalo)
Phone: (716) 652-4704
E-mail: guarunlimited@aol.com

Inventors Alliance of America – Buffalo Chapter
Mark Ellwood
3000 Pearl Street
Olympic Towers, Suite 200
Buffalo, NY 14202
Phone: (716) 842-4561
E-mail: ellwood@netcom.ca

Inventors Alliance of America – Rochester Chapter
Jim Chiello
97 Pinebrook Drive
Rochester, NY 14616
Phone: (716) 225-3750
E-mail: InventNY@aol.com

Long Island Forum for Technology, Inc.
Lisa Carter
111 West main Street
Bay Shore, NY 11706
Ph: (631) 969-3700 or (631) 755-3321 or (516) 755-3321
E-mail: LCarter@lift.org or porlando@lift.org

NY Society of Professional Inventors
Daniel Weiss
Box 216
Farmingdale, NY 11735-9996
Phone: (516) 798-1490
E-mail: dan.weiss.PE@juno.com

Inventors Society of Western New York
Bob Murray
52 Manor Hill Drive.
Fairport, NY 14450
Phone: (585) 223-1225 or (716) 225-6369
E-mail: inventnewyork@aol.com or jchiello@aol.com

Binghamton Inventors Network
Mark Pierson
Phone: (607) 648-4626
E-mail: mvpierson@aol.com

North Carolina

Inventors' Network of the Carolinas
Chip Celley
520 Elliot Street, Suite 300
Charlotte, NC 28202
Phone: (803) 242-0556
E-mail: chipcelley@msn.com

North Dakota

North Dakota Inventors Congress
Michael S. Neustel
2534 South University Drive, Suite 4
Fargo, ND 58103
Phone: (800) 281-7009 or (701) 252-4959
E-mail: neustel@patent-ideas.com
Website: www.ndinventors.com

Ohio

Inventors Network of Greater Akron
John Sovis
1741 Stone Creek Lane
Twinsburgh, OH 44087
Phone: (330) 425-1749

Inventor's Council of Cincinnati
Andrea Brady, President
121 Bradford Drive
Milford, OH 45150
Phone: (513) 831-0664 or (513) 772-9333 or (513) 831-3011
E-mail: InventorsCouncil@fuse.net

Inventors Connection Greater Cleveland
Bill Bazik
PO Box 360804
Strongville, OH 44136
Phone: (216)226-9681 (Cal Wight) or (440) 543-3594
E-mail: icgc@usa.com
Website: members.aol.com/icgc/index.htm

Inventors Network, Inc.
Bob Stonecypher
1275 Kinnear Rd.
Columbus, OH 43212
Phone: (614) 470-0144
E-mail: 13832667@msn.com

Inventors Council of Canton
Frank Fleischer
303 55th Street NW
No. Canton, OH 44720
Phone: (330) 499-1262
E-mail: FFleischer@neo.rr.com or fleisherb@aol.com

Inventors Council of Dayton
George Pierce
PO Box 611
Dayton, OH 45409
Phone: (937) 321-6580 or (937) 293-3073
E-mail: geopierce@earthlink.net
Website: www.daytoninventors.com

Youngstown-Warren Inv. Assn.
Robert J. Herberger
E-mail: rjh@mm-lawyers.com or mm@cisnet.com
500 City Center One - PO Box 500
Youngstown, OH 44501-0500
Phone: (330) 744-4481

Oklahoma

Oklahoma Inventors Congress
William H. Baker
PO Box 57464
Oklahoma City, OK 73157-7464
Phone: (405) 947-5782
Website: www.oklahomainventors.com

Weekend Entrepreneurs
Dale Davis
8102 South Sandusky Avenue
Tulsa, OK 74137
Phone: (918) 664-5831

Oregon

Central Oregon Inventors Group
Marilyn Mallet
61739 Bridge Creek Drive
Bend, OR 97702
Phone: (541) 382-8293
E-mail: mallet9@bendbroadband.com

South Oregon Inventors Council
Nancy Hudson
332 W. 6th St.
SBDC@ S. Oregon State
Medford, OR 97501
Phone: (541)772-3478

South Coast Inventors Group
Lori Capps
2455 Maple Leaf Lane
North Bend, OR 97459
Phone: (541) 756-6866
E-mail: loribdc@uci.net

Blue Mountain Community College Inventors Group
Contact; Jill Pursel
37 SE Dorion Ave.
Pendleton, OR 97801
Phone: (541) 276-6233
E-Mail: jpursel@bluecc.net
Website: www.bizcenter.org

Inventors Group at Umpqua Community College SBDC
251 Woodberry Ln
Roseburg, OR 97470
Contact: Walt Bammann
Phone: (541) 673-8309 (call after 3:00 p.m.)
E-mail: wbamman@wizzards.net

Pennsylvania

American Society of Inventors
PO Box 58426
Philadelphia, PA 19102-5426)
Phone: (215) 546-6601
E-mail: hskillman@ddhs.com
Website: www.asoi.org

Central Pennsylvania Inventors Assn.
Scott Pickford
117 N. 20th Street
Camp Hill, PA 17011
Phone: (717) 763-5742
E-mail: S1Pickford@aol.com

Pennsylvania Inventors Assn.
Jerry T. Gorniak
2317 East 43rd St.
Erie, PA 16510
Phone: (814) 825-5820
E-mail: dhbutler@velocity.net
Website: www.painventors.org

Puerto Rico

Puerto Rico Inventors Association
Bill Diaz
PO Box 1081
Saint Just, PR 00978
Phone: (787) 760-5074
E-mail: acuhost@novacomm-inc.com

Rhode Island

The Center for Design & Business
Cheryl A. Daria, Director
20 Washington Place
Providence, RI 02903
Phone: (401) 454-6108
E-mail: cfaria@risd.edu

South Carolina

Carolina Inventors Council
Marion Kobusch
108 Monarch Place
Taylors, SC 29687
Phone: (864) 268-9892 or (864) 859-0066
E-mail: mkundercover1@aol.com or john17@home.com

Inventors & Entrepreneurs Association of South Carolina
Charles Sprouse
PO Box 4123
Greenville, SC 29608
Phone: (864) 244-1045

South Dakota

South Dakota Inventors Congress
Kent Rufer
PO Box 2220, SDSU-EERC
Brookings, SD 57007
Phone: (605) 688-4184
E-mail: kent_rufer@sdstate.edu

Tennessee

Tennessee Inventors Assn. (East Tennessee)
Anne Alexeff, President
PO Box 11225
Knoxville, TN 37939-1225
Phone: (865) 981-2927 or (423) 869-8138
E-mail: ialexeff@comcast.net or bealaj@aol.com
Website: www.uscni.com/tia

Inventors' Association of Middle Tennessee
and South Kentucky
Marshal Frazer
3908 Trimble Rd.
Nashville, TN 37215
Phone: (615) 665-1525 or (615) 269-4346
E-mail: timr@dtccom.net
Website: www.iamt.us

Texas

Amarillo Inventors Association
Paul Kiefer, President
7000 West 45th
Amarillo, TX 79109
Phone: (806) 352-6085
E-mail: KIEFER7000@aol.com

Austin Inventors & Entrepreneurs Association
Austin, TX
Jesse Redman, President
E-mail: jredman@austin.rr.com
Website: www.austininventors.org

Houston Inventors Association
Ken Roddy
2916 West TC Jester #100
Houston, TX 77018
Phone: (713) 686-7676 or (713) 523-3923
E-mail: kenroddy@nol.net or mcalicat@netscape.net
Website: www.inventors.org

Laredo Inventors Association
Jorge Guerra
210 Palm Circle
Laredo, TX 78041
Phone: (956) 725-5863

Tarrant County Inventors
Danelle Ellis
E-mail: Danelle.ellis@sbcglobal.net

Technology Advocates of San Antonio
Inventors &Entrepreneurs SIG
Mr. John Poston
10507 Auldine Drive
San Antonio, TX 78250
Phone: (210) 525-8510 or (210) 724-2545or (210) 491-6554
E-mail: jposton@jbengineering.com or hoh1@flash.net
Website: www.inventsanantonio.com

Texas Inventors Association
Robert Wise
PO Box 251248
Plano, TX 75025
E-mail: rewise1@comcast.net
Website: www.txinventors.com

Utah

University of Utah
Engineering Experiment Station
Janeen Bennion
1495 East 100 South, Room 138
Salt Lake City, UT 84112
Phone: (801) 581-6348

Vermont

Inventors Network of Vermont
Dave Dionne
4 Park Street
Springfield, VT 05156
Phone: (802) 885-5100 or (802) 885-8178 or (802) 885-8094
E-mail: comtu@turbont.net

Invent Vermont
Norman Etkind
PO Box 82
Woodbury, VT 05681
Phone: (802) 472-8741
E-mail: Netkind@att.net
Website: www.inventvermont.com

Virginia

Blue Ridge Inventor's Club
Mac Woodward
PO Box 6701
Charlottesville, VA 22906-6701
Phone: (434) 973-3708 or (804) 973-3708
E-mail: mac@luckycat.com
Website: www.inventorclub.org

Association for Science, Technology & Innovation
Robert Adams
PO Box 1242
Arlington, VA 22210
Phone: (703) 241-2850

Washington

Inventors Network
Rick Aydelott
PO Box 5575
Vancouver, WA 98668
Phone: (503) 239-8299

Whidbey Island Inventor Network
Matthew Swett
PO Box 1026
Langley, WA 98260
Phone: (360) 678-0269
E-mail: wiin@whidbey.com
Website: www2.whidbey.net/wiin

Northwest Inventors Guild
Port Townsend, WA
Phone: (360) 385-7038
E-mail: aero1@waypt.com

Tri-Cities Enterprise Association
Dallas Breamer
2000 Logston Blvd.
Richland, WA 99352
Phone: (509) 375-3268

Wisconsin

Central Wisconsin Inventors Association
Steve Sorenson
PO Box 915
Manawa, WI 54949
Phone: (920) 982-3323 or (920) 596-3092
E-mail: dr.heat@excite.com or drheat@excite.com

Inventors Network of Wisconsin
Jeff Hitzler
1066 Saint Paul Street
Green Bay, WI 54304
Phone: (920) 429-0331
E-mail: inventorgb@msn.com or jhitzler@megtec.com

Incubator Program
David Fry
University of WI-Stout
328 Fryklund Hall
Menomonie, WI 54751
Phone: (715) 232-5041
E-mail: fryd@uwstout.edu

Innovative Minds of Wisconsin
Craig Brown
1215 Norway Drive
Mosinee, WI 54455
Phone: (715) 693-3235
E-mail: InnovativeMindsWisconsin@yahoo.com

Appendix B

Helpful links

General Resources

The Academy of Applied Sciences -
www.aas-world.org

The Academy is recognized nationally as an educational resource center offering enrichment programs for students, and professional development for teachers and educational administrators.

The Canadian Innovation Centre
www.innovationcentre.ca

CI is Canada's leading organization dedicated to assisting inventors and innovative companies. Our range of services includes invention evaluation, technology due diligence, market research, and education programs.

Inventors' Digest Magazine
www.inventorsdigest.com

The United States only magazine dedicated to providing informative articles for the individual inventor.

The United Inventors Association of the USA
www.uiausa.org

The United Inventors Association (UIA) is a tax-exempt, not for profit corporation formed in 1990 solely for educational purposes. If you're an independent inventor, or an inventors networking group, or someone that provides services for new product development, this is the community center you've been looking for.

Ask the Inventors!
www.asktheinventors.com

Great idea? What next? Are you looking for trustworthy help to get your invention developed, patented and on the market? We know how you feel; we have been right there! Now, as successful inventors, we want to help you to find success without being scammed by invention promoters. Developing, protecting and marketing can be confusing, but we are here with answers!

Inventors HQ
www.inventorshq.com
Helping inventors from around the world to get their products from the garage to the marketplace for the least amount of out-of-pocket money as humanly possible.

Patents, Trademarks & Patent Searching

Dirt Cheap Patents
www.dirtcheappatents.com

Need professional help writing your patent on your relatively simple invention but money is an issue? Try Dirt Cheap Patents. There is a coupon for a free consultation with a patent agent in the coupon section at the back of this book.

Patent Search International
www.patentsearchinternational.com/

"My job is to help thinkers become doers..." Ron Brown, President Patent Search International. Ron says, "I started Patent Search International because I saw that inventors had two needs that weren't being provided: first, they needed to save money; and second, they had a right to a reliable assessment of their invention without being ripped-off. Every inventor really has to have a patent search done, otherwise you risk losing a lot of money. But a lot of inventors don't know that they don't have to pay as much to get the job done right. That's the whole aim of Patent Search International." (There is a coupon for PSI for a $25 dollar discount in the coupon section at the back of this book.)

Neustel Law
www.neustel.com

A patent law office that helps businesses and inventors protect their intellectual property assets including patents, trademarks and copyrights. Michael Neustel is a U.S. Registered Patent Attorney with a Bachelor of Science in Electrical Engineering and is licensed to practice in front of the United States Patent and Trademark Office USPTO).

Patent Hunter

www.patenthunter.com

This is a must-have for serious inventors. This software program, created by U. S. Patent Attorney Michael S. Neustel, allows you to download multiple patents at the same time from the USPTO database. You now have patents and images available for viewing at your convenience.

PatentPro
www.patentpro.us

Creates the patent application for you! It even helps you write the claims like a seasoned patent attorney! Guides you through the patent process automatically. Generates all your forms and helps you to prepare drawings. Contains all the materials needed to file your own complete patent application with the United States Patent and Trademark Office. Use it over and over again to file additional patent applications. Unlike other patent software that prepares only a provisional application, a patent application prepared with PatentPro is reviewed by a trained Examiner at the Patent Office who conducts a prior art search for you. A huge savings over Attorneys that charge $5,000 per application

Patent Wizard
http://www.patentwizard.com

This software, created by U. S. Patent Attorney Michael S. Neustel, lets independent inventors prepare and file provisional patent applications that look like they were done by an attorney (a real plus with the USPTO!)

Patent Ease
inventorprise.com/Merchant2/merchant.
mv?Screen=PROD&Store_Code=IVP&Product_Code=UPC83755800102

This software provides guidance and ease in writing your own patent applications. The cost is $299 but if you give them the following coupon number (R4ATIIPP102) you will receive a $50 discount!

United States Patent and Trademark Office
www.uspto.gov

AlternaTIFF
alternatiff.com
Free download for viewing patent drawings on USPTO website

InterneTIFF
www.internetiff.com
Free download for viewing patent drawings on USPTO website

Instructions for doing a classification patent search on the USPTO website:
www.uspto.gov/web/offices/ac/ido/ptdl/step7.htm

Free guide for performing preliminary patent search on USPTO website:
asktheinventors.com/Books/patentsearch.htm

Free download for Adobe Acrobat Reader:
www.download-it-free.com/acrobat/

USPTO Disclosure Document Program

United States Patent and Trademark Office's Disclosure Document program:

www.uspto.gov/web/offices/pac/disdo.html

Cover page for Disclosure Document Program:
www.uspto.gov/web/forms/sb0095.pdf

Prototypes

Plastic Prototypes
www.plasticprototypes.net

Book and video with easy instructions for making your own good-looking plastic prototype

Product Evaluations

Innovation Institute
www.wini2.com

Source for reasonably priced product evaluations

United Inventors' Association's Innovation Assessment Program
www.uiausa.com/Services/IAP/UIAIAP.htm

Reasonably priced product evaluation.

Harvey Reese and Associates
www.money4ideas.com

Legitimate product licensing agents.

University of Wisconsin Innovation Service Center
www.academics.uww.edu/business/innovate/contact_us.htm

Source for thorough professional product evaluations

Scam Avoidance

Federal Trade Commission
https://rn.ftc.gov/pls/dod/wsolcq$.startup?Z_ORG_CODE=PU01

For filing a complaint against an invention promotion company

United States Patent & Trademark Office
www.uspto.gov/web/forms/2048.pdf

For filing a complaint against an invention promotion company

RJ Riley's Scam watchdog website
www.inventored.org

Lists companies who have had complaints lodged against them.

Funding

National Institute of Standards and Technology
www.nist.gov/public_affairs/grants.htm

The NIST offers grants.

About.com- How to get New Ideas Funded
inventors.about.com/od/gettingthemoney

Deal Flow Venture Capital Firms & Angel Investors
www.dealflow.com

Department of Energy Inventions and Innovations
www.oit.doe.gov

On this site you will find grants for research and development of energy related inventions.

National Science Foundation Grants & awards
www.nsf.gov/home/grants.htm

Small Business Administration
www.sbaonline.sba.gov/hotlist/procure.html

Student Programs for Invention Funding
inventors.about.com/od/competitionsprize

VFinance.com Directory
www.vfinance.com

Directory of 1,800 Venture Capital Firms and 23,000 angel Investors

Manufacturing & Licensing

The Thomas Register
www.thomasnet.com

Listings of manufacturers according to the types of items they manufacture. Available in a 20 volume set at public libraries everywhere and in a more limited version online. When you are ready to locate possible licensees this is one of the first places you should visit.

Licensing Executives Society
www.usa-canada.les.org

Attorneys who are experts in writing and negotiating license agreements

Off shore Manufacturing

EGT Global Trading
www.hometown.aol.com/egtglobaltrading

Edie Tolchin holds a customs Broker License, and specializes in manufacturing and importing services for inventions of textiles and sewn items, bags, baby & fashion accessories, arts & crafts and small household items. If your item fits into her categories and you want your product priced and produced offshore for bottom dollar Edie is the person to contact!

Toy resources

The Toy Industry Association
www.toy-tia.org

Women in Toys Association
www.womenintoys.com/profile_PattyBecker.html

American Specialty Toys Retail Association
www.astratoy.org/i4a/pages/index.cfm?pageid=1

Playthings Magazine
www.playthings.com

Games Quarterly
www.gamesquarterly.net

The Toy Industry Association's annual Toy Fair in New York City
http://www.toy-tia.org/Content/NavigationMenu TIA_Trade_Shows_ and_Events/American_International_TOY_FAIR/American_ International_TOY_FAIR1.htm

Toys n Games Show, TGIF
www.toysngames.com/tgif/tgifover.htm

Non-disclosure Documents

Free non-disclosure documents to print for your use
`asktheinventors.com/nondisclosure.htm`

Appendix C
Patent & Trademark Depository Libraries

Alabama
    Auburn University Libraries (205) 844-1737
    Birmingham Public Library (205) 226-3620

Alaska
    Anchorage: Z.J. Loussac Public Library (907) 562-7323

Arizona
    Tempe: Noble Library, Arizona State University (602) 965-7010

Arkansas
    Little Rock: Arkansas State Library (501) 682-2053

California
    Los Angeles Public Library (213) 228-7220
    Sacramento: California State Library (916) 654-0069
    San Diego Public Library (619) 236-5813
    San Francisco Public Library (415) 557-4488
    Sunnyvale Patent Clearinghouse (408) 730-7290

Colorado
    Denver Public Library (303) 640-8847

Connecticut
    New Haven: Free Public Library (203) 946-7452
    Hartford: Hartford Public Library (860) 543-8628

Delaware
    Newark: University of Delaware Library (302) 831-2965

District of Columbia
    Howard University Libraries (202) 806-7252

Florida
Fort Lauderdale: Broward County Main Library (305) 357-7444
Miami-Dade Public Library (305) 375-2665
Orlando: University of Central Florida Libraries (407) 823-2562
Tampa Campus Library, University of South florida (813) 974-2726

Georgia
Atlanta: Price Gilbert Memorial Library, Georgia Institute of
Technology (404) 894-4508

Hawaii
Honolulu: Hawaii State Public Library System (808) 586-3477

Idaho
Moscow: University of Idaho Library (208) 885-6235

Illinois
Chicago Public Library (312) 747-4450

Indiana
Indianapolis-Marion County Public Library (317) 269-1741
West Lafayette: Siegesmund Engineering Library, Purdue University
(317) 494-2872

Iowa
Des Moines: State Library of Iowa (515) 281-4118

Kansas
Wichita: Ablah Library, Wichita State Library (316) 689-3155

Kentucky
Louisville Free Public Library (502) 574-1611

Louisiana
Baton Rouge: Troy H. Middleton Library, Louisiana State University
(504) 388-8875

Maine
Orono: Raymond H. Fogler Library, University of Maine
(207) 581-1691

Maryland
  College Park: Engineering and Physical Sciences Library, University of Maryland (301) 405-9157

Massachusetts
  Amherst: Physical Sciences Library, University of Massachusetts (413) 545-1370
  Boston Public Library (617) 536-5400, ext. 265

Michigan
  Ann Arbor: Media Union, University of Michigan (734) 647-5735
  Big Rapids: Abigail S. Timme Library, Ferris State University (616) 592-3602
  Detroit Public Library (313) 833-3379

Minnesota
  Minneapolis Public Library and Information Center (612) 630-6120

Mississippi
  Jackson: Mississippi Library Commission (601) 961-4111

Missouri
  Kansas City: Linda Hall Library (816) 363-4600
  St. Louis Public Library (314) 241-2288, ext. 390

Montana
  Butte: Montana college of Mineral Science and Technology Library (406) 496-4281

Nebraska
  Lincoln: Engineering Library, University of Nebraska-Lincoln (402) 472-3411

Nevada
  Las Vegas: Clark County Library (Not Yet Operational)
  Reno: University of Nevada-Reno Library (702) 784-6500

New Hampshire
  Concord: New Hampshire State Library (603) 271-2239

New Jersey
Newark Public Library (973) 733-7779
Piscataway: Library of Science and Medicine, Rutgers University (908) 445-2895

New Mexico
Albuquerque: University of New Mexico General Library (505) 277-4412

New York
Albany: New York State Library (518) 474-5355
Buffalo and Erie County Public Library (716) 858-7101
New York Public Library (the Research Libraries) (212) 592-7000
Rochester: Center Library of Rochester and Monroe County (716) 428-8110
Stony Brook: Melville Library, Room 1101, SUNY at Stony Brook (516) 632-7148

Ohio
Akron: Akron-Summit County Public Library (330) 643-9075
Cincinnati: Public Library of Cincinnati & Hamilton City (513) 369-6932
Cleveland: Cleveland Public Library (216) 623-2870
Columbus: Ohio State University (614) 292-3022
Dayton: Wright State University (937) 775-3521
Toledo: Toledo/Lucas County Public Library (419) 259-5209

Oklahoma
Stillwater: Edmon Low Library, Oklahoma State University (405) 744-7086

Oregon
Portland: Paul L. Boley Law Library, Lewis & Clark College (503) 768-6786

Pennsylvania
Philadelphia: The Free Library of Philadelphia (215) 686-5331
Pittsburgh: The Carnegie Library of Pittsburgh (412) 622-3138
University Park: Paterno Library, Pennsylvania State University (814) 865-6369

Puerto Rico
Bayamón: Learning Resource Center, Bayamón Campus, University of Puerto Rico (787) 786-5225
Mayagüez: General Library, Mayagüez Campus, University of Puerto Rico (787) 832-4040 Ext. 2307

Rhode Island
Providence: Providence Public Library (401) 455-8027

South Carolina
Clemson: R. M. Cooper Library, Clemson University (864) 656-3024

South Dakota
Rapid City: Devereaux Library, South Dakota School of Mines and Technology (605) 394-1275

Tennessee
Nashville: Stevenson Science & Engineering Library, Vanderbilt University (615) 322-2717

Texas
Austin: McKinney Engineering Library, ECJ 1.300, The University of Texas at Austin (512) 495-4500
College Station: Texas A&M University Libraries (979) 458-1819
Dallas: Dallas Public Library (214) 670-1468
Houston: Fondren Library - MS 225, Rice University (713) 348-5483
Lubbock: Texas Tech University Library (806) 742-2282
San Antonio: San Antonio Public Library (210) 207-2500

Utah
Salt Lake City: Marriott Library, University of Utah (801) 581-8394

Vermont
Burlington: Bailey/Howe Library, University of Vermont (802) 656-2542

Virginia
Richmond: James Branch Cabell Library, Virginia, Commonwealth University (804) 828-1101

Washington
    Seattle: Engineering Library, University of Washington
    (206) 543-0740

West Virginia
    Morgantown: Evansdale Library, West Virginia University
    304) 293-4695, Ext. 5113

Wisconsin
    Madison: Kurt F. Wendt Library, University of Wisconsin-Madison
    (608) 262-6845
    Milwaukee Public Library (414) 286-3051

Wyoming
    Cheyenne: Wyoming State Library (307) 777-7281

Index

About the Authors

Sisters **Barbara Russell Pitts** and **Mary Russell Sarao** are co-authors of "The Everything Inventions and Patents Book," which was published in December 2005 by Adams Media. Barbara has written for the United Inventors' Association Newsletter and the Ask the Inventors website, www. asktheinventors.com, an information service they offer at no charge for inventors. Mary has written two popular e-books, "Super Easy Guide to Step-by-Step Patent Searching Online" and "Create a Compelling Presentation for your Invention," that are offered without cost to visitors to their website, www.asktheinventors.com. She has also written for that website and for the Texas Inventors' Association Website, www.txinventors.com.

Successful inventors and recognized experts on the subject, Barbara and Mary have lectured extensively on the different areas of inventing and marketing at seminars, workshops and organizations around the country as well as appearing on radio and television talk shows. In 2001, they were featured inventors in the documentary film, "The Big Idea."

Barbara has served on the board of directors and as secretary of the executive committee of the United Inventors Association and is a past president and current board member of the Texas Inventors' Association. Mary has served on the Board of Directors of the United Inventors Association and is a past president and current board member of the Texas Inventors' Association. In July 2003 and again in January 2006 Barbara and Mary were the subject of articles in the Dallas Morning News about their passion for assisting novice inventors. The first article was picked up by the wire services and carried in newspapers nationwide.

Both are native Oklahomans who now live in the Dallas, Texas area.

Inventing on a Shoestring Budget™! **Inventing** on a Shoestring Budget™! **Inventing** on a string Budget! **Inventing** on a Shoestring Budget™! **Inventing** on a Shoestring Budget™! **Invent** **Inventing** on a Shoestring Budget™! **Inventing** on a Shoestring Budget™! **Inventing** on a string Budget! **Inventing** on a Shoestring Budget™! **Inventing** on a Shoestring Budget™! **Invent** **Inventing** on a Shoestring Budget™! **Inventing** on a Shoestring Budget™! **Inventing** on a string Budget! **Inventing** on a Shoestring Budget™! **Inventing** on a Shoestring Budget™! **Invent** **Inventing** on a Shoestring Budget™! **Inventing** on a Shoestring Budget™! **Inventing** on a string Budget! **Inventing** on a Shoestring Budget™! **Inventing** on a Shoestring Budget™! **Invent** **Inventing** on a Shoestring Budget™! **Inventing** on a Shoestring Budget™! **Inventing** on a string Budget! **Inventing** on a Shoestring Budget™! **Inventing** on a Shoestring Budget™! **Invent** **Inventing** on a Shoestring Budget™! **Inventing** on a Shoestring Budget™! **Inventing** on a string Budget! **Inventing** on a Shoestring Budget™! **Inventing** on a Shoestring Budget™! **Invent** **Inventing** on a Shoestring Budget™! **Inventing** on a Shoestring Budget™! **Inventing** on a string Budget! **Inventing** on a Shoestring Budget™! **Inventing** on a Shoestring Budget™! **Invent** **Inventing** on a Shoestring Budget™! **Inventing** on a Shoestring Budget™! **Inventing** on a string Budget! **Inventing** on a Shoestring Budget™! **Inventing** on a Shoestring Budget™! **Invent** **Inventing** on a Shoestring Budget™! **Inventing** on a Shoestring Budget™! **Inventing** on a string Budget! **Inventing** on a Shoestring Budget™! **Inventing** on a Shoestring Budget™! **Invent** **Inventing** on a Shoestring Budget™! **Inventing** on a Shoestring Budget™! **Inventing** on a string Budget! **Inventing** on a Shoestring Budget™! **Inventing** on a Shoestring Budget™! **Invent** **Inventing** on a Shoestring Budget™! **Inventing** on a Shoestring Budget™! **Inventing** on a string Budget! **Inventing** on a Shoestring Budget™! **Inventing** on a Shoestring Budget™! **Invent** **Inventing** on a Shoestring Budget™! **Inventing** on a Shoestring Budget™! **Inventing** on a string Budget! **Inventing** on a Shoestring Budget™! **Inventing** on a Shoestring Budget™! **Invent** **Inventing** on a Shoestring Budget™! **Inventing** on a Shoestring Budget™! **Inventing** on a string Budget! **Inventing** on a Shoestring Budget™! **Inventing** on a Shoestring Budget™! **Invent** **Inventing** on a Shoestring Budget™! **Inventing** on a Shoestring Budget™! **Inventing** on a

Inventing on a Shoestring Budget™! **Inventing** on a Shoestring Budget™! **Inventing** on a string Budget! **Inventing** on a Shoestring Budget™! **Inventing** on a Shoestring Budget™! **Invent Inventing** on a Shoestring Budget™! **Inventing** on a Shoestring Budget™! **Inventing** on a string Budget! **Inventing** on a Shoestring Budget™! **Inventing** on a Shoestring Budget™! **Invent Inventing** on a Shoestring Budget™! **Inventing** on a Shoestring Budget™! **Inventing** on a string Budget! **Inventing** on a Shoestring Budget™! **Inventing** on a Shoestring Budget™! **Invent Inventing** on a Shoestring Budget™! **Inventing** on a Shoestring Budget™! **Inventing** on a string Budget! **Inventing** on a Shoestring Budget™! **Inventing** on a Shoestring Budget™! **Invent Inventing** on a Shoestring Budget™! **Inventing** on a Shoestring Budget™! **Inventing** on a string Budget! **Inventing** on a Shoestring Budget™! **Inventing** on a Shoestring Budget™! **Invent Inventing** on a Shoestring Budget™! **Inventing** on a Shoestring Budget™! **Inventing** on a string Budget! **Inventing** on a Shoestring Budget™! **Inventing** on a Shoestring Budget™! **Invent Inventing** on a Shoestring Budget™! **Inventing** on a Shoestring Budget™! **Inventing** on a string Budget! **Inventing** on a Shoestring Budget™! **Inventing** on a Shoestring Budget™! **Invent Inventing** on a Shoestring Budget™! **Inventing** on a Shoestring Budget™! **Inventing** on a string Budget! **Inventing** on a Shoestring Budget™! **Inventing** on a Shoestring Budget™! **Invent Inventing** on a Shoestring Budget™! **Inventing** on a Shoestring Budget™! **Inventing** on a string Budget! **Inventing** on a Shoestring Budget™! **Inventing** on a Shoestring Budget™! **Invent Inventing** on a Shoestring Budget™! **Inventing** on a Shoestring Budget™! **Inventing** on a string Budget! **Inventing** on a Shoestring Budget™! **Inventing** on a Shoestring Budget™! **Invent Inventing** on a Shoestring Budget™! **Inventing** on a Shoestring Budget™! **Inventing** on a string Budget! **Inventing** on a Shoestring Budget™! **Inventing** on a Shoestring Budget™! **Invent Inventing** on a Shoestring Budget™! **Inventing** on a Shoestring Budget™! **Inventing** on a string Budget! **Inventing** on a Shoestring Budget™! **Inventing** on a Shoestring Budget™! **Invent Inventing** on a Shoestring Budget™! **Inventing** on a Shoestring Budget™! **Inventing** on a string Budget! **Inventing** on a Shoestring Budget™! **Inventing** on a Shoestring Budget™! **Invent Inventing** on a Shoestring Budget™! **Inventing** on a Shoestring Budget™! **Inventing** on a string Budget! **Inventing** on a Shoestring Budget™! **Inventing** on a Shoestring Budget™! **Invent Inventing** on a Shoestring Budget™! **Inventing** on a Shoestring Budget™! **Inventing** on a string Budget! **Inventing** on a Shoestring Budget™! **Inventing** on a Shoestring Budget™! **Invent Inventing** on a Shoestring Budget™! **Inventing** on a Shoestring Budget™! **Inventing** on a string Budget! **Inventing** on a Shoestring Budget™! **Inventing** on a Shoestring Budget™! **Invent Inventing** on a Shoestring Budget™! **Inventing** on a Shoestring Budget™! **Inventing** on a

Inventing on a Shoestring Budget™! **Inventing** on a Shoestring Budget™! **Inventing** on a string Budget! **Inventing** on a Shoestring Budget™! **Inventing** on a Shoestring Budget™! **Invent Inventing** on a Shoestring Budget™! **Inventing** on a Shoestring Budget™! **Inventing** on a string Budget! **Inventing** on a Shoestring Budget™! **Inventing** on a Shoestring Budget™! **Invent Inventing** on a Shoestring Budget™! **Inventing** on a Shoestring Budget™! **Inventing** on a string Budget! **Inventing** on a Shoestring Budget™! **Inventing** on a Shoestring Budget™! **Invent Inventing** on a Shoestring Budget™! **Inventing** on a Shoestring Budget™! **Inventing** on a string Budget! **Inventing** on a Shoestring Budget™! **Inventing** on a Shoestring Budget™! **Invent Inventing** on a Shoestring Budget™! **Inventing** on a Shoestring Budget™! **Inventing** on a string Budget! **Inventing** on a Shoestring Budget™! **Inventing** on a Shoestring Budget™! **Invent Inventing** on a Shoestring Budget™! **Inventing** on a Shoestring Budget™! **Inventing** on a string Budget! **Inventing** on a Shoestring Budget™! **Inventing** on a Shoestring Budget™! **Invent Inventing** on a Shoestring Budget™! **Inventing** on a Shoestring Budget™! **Inventing** on a string Budget! **Inventing** on a Shoestring Budget™! **Inventing** on a Shoestring Budget™! **Invent Inventing** on a Shoestring Budget™! **Inventing** on a Shoestring Budget™! **Inventing** on a string Budget! **Inventing** on a Shoestring Budget™! **Inventing** on a Shoestring Budget™! **Invent Inventing** on a Shoestring Budget™! **Inventing** on a Shoestring Budget™! **Inventing** on a string Budget! **Inventing** on a Shoestring Budget™! **Inventing** on a Shoestring Budget™! **Invent Inventing** on a Shoestring Budget™! **Inventing** on a Shoestring Budget™! **Inventing** on a string Budget! **Inventing** on a Shoestring Budget™! **Inventing** on a Shoestring Budget™! **Invent Inventing** on a Shoestring Budget™! **Inventing** on a Shoestring Budget™! **Inventing** on a string Budget! **Inventing** on a Shoestring Budget™! **Inventing** on a Shoestring Budget™! **Invent Inventing** on a Shoestring Budget™! **Inventing** on a Shoestring Budget™! **Inventing** on a string Budget! **Inventing** on a Shoestring Budget™! **Inventing** on a Shoestring Budget™! **Invent Inventing** on a Shoestring Budget™! **Inventing** on a Shoestring Budget™! **Inventing** on a string Budget! **Inventing** on a Shoestring Budget™! **Inventing** on a Shoestring Budget™! **Invent Inventing** on a Shoestring Budget™! **Inventing** on a Shoestring Budget™! **Inventing** on a string Budget! **Inventing** on a Shoestring Budget™! **Inventing** on a Shoestring Budget™! **Invent Inventing** on a Shoestring Budget™! **Inventing** on a Shoestring Budget™! **Inventing** on a

Inventing on a Shoestring Budget"! **Inventing** on a Shoestring Budget"! **Inventing** on a string Budget! **Inventing** on a Shoestring Budget"! **Inventing** on a Shoestring Budget"! **Invent** **Inventing** on a Shoestring Budget"! **Inventing** on a Shoestring Budget"! **Inventing** on a string Budget! **Inventing** on a Shoestring Budget"! **Inventing** on a Shoestring Budget"! **Invent** **Inventing** on a Shoestring Budget"! **Inventing** on a Shoestring Budget"! **Inventing** on a string Budget! **Inventing** on a Shoestring Budget"! **Inventing** on a Shoestring Budget"! **Invent** **Inventing** on a Shoestring Budget"! **Inventing** on a Shoestring Budget"! **Inventing** on a string Budget! **Inventing** on a Shoestring Budget"! **Inventing** on a Shoestring Budget"! **Invent** **Inventing** on a Shoestring Budget"! **Inventing** on a Shoestring Budget"! **Inventing** on a string Budget! **Inventing** on a Shoestring Budget"! **Inventing** on a Shoestring Budget"! **Invent** **Inventing** on a Shoestring Budget"! **Inventing** on a Shoestring Budget"! **Inventing** on a string Budget! **Inventing** on a Shoestring Budget"! **Inventing** on a Shoestring Budget"! **Invent** **Inventing** on a Shoestring Budget"! **Inventing** on a Shoestring Budget"! **Inventing** on a string Budget! **Inventing** on a Shoestring Budget"! **Inventing** on a Shoestring Budget"! **Invent** **Inventing** on a Shoestring Budget"! **Inventing** on a Shoestring Budget"! **Inventing** on a string Budget! **Inventing** on a Shoestring Budget"! **Inventing** on a Shoestring Budget"! **Invent** **Inventing** on a Shoestring Budget"! **Inventing** on a Shoestring Budget"! **Inventing** on a string Budget! **Inventing** on a Shoestring Budget"! **Inventing** on a Shoestring Budget"! **Invent** **Inventing** on a Shoestring Budget"! **Inventing** on a Shoestring Budget"! **Inventing** on a string Budget! **Inventing** on a Shoestring Budget"! **Inventing** on a Shoestring Budget"! **Invent** **Inventing** on a Shoestring Budget"! **Inventing** on a Shoestring Budget"! **Inventing** on a string Budget! **Inventing** on a Shoestring Budget"! **Inventing** on a Shoestring Budget"! **Invent** **Inventing** on a Shoestring Budget"! **Inventing** on a Shoestring Budget"! **Inventing** on a string Budget! **Inventing** on a Shoestring Budget"! **Inventing** on a Shoestring Budget"! **Invent** **Inventing** on a Shoestring Budget"! **Inventing** on a Shoestring Budget"! **Inventing** on a string Budget! **Inventing** on a Shoestring Budget"! **Inventing** on a Shoestring Budget"! **Invent** **Inventing** on a Shoestring Budget"! **Inventing** on a Shoestring Budget"! **Inventing** on a

Inventing on a Shoestring Budget™! **Inventing** on a Shoestring Budget™! **Inventing** on a string Budget! **Inventing** on a Shoestring Budget™! **Inventing** on a Shoestring Budget™! **Invent Inventing** on a Shoestring Budget™! **Inventing** on a Shoestring Budget™! **Inventing** on a string Budget! **Inventing** on a Shoestring Budget™! **Inventing** on a Shoestring Budget™! **Invent Inventing** on a Shoestring Budget™! **Inventing** on a Shoestring Budget™! **Inventing** on a string Budget! **Inventing** on a Shoestring Budget™! **Inventing** on a Shoestring Budget™! **Invent Inventing** on a Shoestring Budget™! **Inventing** on a Shoestring Budget™! **Inventing** on a string Budget! **Inventing** on a Shoestring Budget™! **Inventing** on a Shoestring Budget™! **Invent Inventing** on a Shoestring Budget™! **Inventing** on a Shoestring Budget™! **Inventing** on a string Budget! **Inventing** on a Shoestring Budget™! **Inventing** on a Shoestring Budget™! **Invent Inventing** on a Shoestring Budget™! **Inventing** on a Shoestring Budget™! **Inventing** on a string Budget! **Inventing** on a Shoestring Budget™! **Inventing** on a Shoestring Budget™! **Invent Inventing** on a Shoestring Budget™! **Inventing** on a Shoestring Budget™! **Inventing** on a string Budget! **Inventing** on a Shoestring Budget™! **Inventing** on a Shoestring Budget™! **Invent Inventing** on a Shoestring Budget™! **Inventing** on a Shoestring Budget™! **Inventing** on a string Budget! **Inventing** on a Shoestring Budget™! **Inventing** on a Shoestring Budget™! **Invent Inventing** on a Shoestring Budget™! **Inventing** on a Shoestring Budget™! **Inventing** on a string Budget! **Inventing** on a Shoestring Budget™! **Inventing** on a Shoestring Budget™! **Invent Inventing** on a Shoestring Budget™! **Inventing** on a Shoestring Budget™! **Inventing** on a string Budget! **Inventing** on a Shoestring Budget™! **Inventing** on a Shoestring Budget™! **Invent Inventing** on a Shoestring Budget™! **Inventing** on a Shoestring Budget™! **Inventing** on a string Budget! **Inventing** on a Shoestring Budget™! **Inventing** on a Shoestring Budget™! **Invent Inventing** on a Shoestring Budget™! **Inventing** on a Shoestring Budget™! **Inventing** on a string Budget! **Inventing** on a Shoestring Budget™! **Inventing** on a Shoestring Budget™! **Invent Inventing** on a Shoestring Budget™! **Inventing** on a Shoestring Budget™! **Inventing** on a string Budget! **Inventing** on a Shoestring Budget™! **Inventing** on a Shoestring Budget™! **Invent Inventing** on a Shoestring Budget™! **Inventing** on a Shoestring Budget™! **Inventing** on a

Inventing on a Shoestring Budget!™ **Inventing** on a Shoestring Budget!™ **Inventing** on a string Budget! **Inventing** on a Shoestring Budget!™ **Inventing** on a Shoestring Budget!™ **Invent Inventing** on a Shoestring Budget!™ **Inventing** on a Shoestring Budget!™ **Inventing** on a string Budget! **Inventing** on a Shoestring Budget!™ **Inventing** on a Shoestring Budget!™ **Invent Inventing** on a Shoestring Budget!™ **Inventing** on a Shoestring Budget!™ **Inventing** on a string Budget! **Inventing** on a Shoestring Budget!™ **Inventing** on a Shoestring Budget!™ **Invent Inventing** on a Shoestring Budget!™ **Inventing** on a Shoestring Budget!™ **Inventing** on a string Budget! **Inventing** on a Shoestring Budget!™ **Inventing** on a Shoestring Budget!™ **Invent Inventing** on a Shoestring Budget!™ **Inventing** on a Shoestring Budget!™ **Inventing** on a string Budget! **Inventing** on a Shoestring Budget!™ **Inventing** on a Shoestring Budget!™ **Invent Inventing** on a Shoestring Budget!™ **Inventing** on a Shoestring Budget!™ **Inventing** on a string Budget! **Inventing** on a Shoestring Budget!™ **Inventing** on a Shoestring Budget!™ **Invent Inventing** on a Shoestring Budget!™ **Inventing** on a Shoestring Budget!™ **Inventing** on a string Budget! **Inventing** on a Shoestring Budget!™ **Inventing** on a Shoestring Budget!™ **Invent Inventing** on a Shoestring Budget!™ **Inventing** on a Shoestring Budget!™ **Inventing** on a string Budget! **Inventing** on a Shoestring Budget!™ **Inventing** on a Shoestring Budget!™ **Invent Inventing** on a Shoestring Budget!™ **Inventing** on a Shoestring Budget!™ **Inventing** on a string Budget! **Inventing** on a Shoestring Budget!™ **Inventing** on a Shoestring Budget!™ **Invent Inventing** on a Shoestring Budget!™ **Inventing** on a Shoestring Budget!™ **Inventing** on a string Budget! **Inventing** on a Shoestring Budget!™ **Inventing** on a Shoestring Budget!™ **Invent Inventing** on a Shoestring Budget!™ **Inventing** on a Shoestring Budget!™ **Inventing** on a string Budget! **Inventing** on a Shoestring Budget!™ **Inventing** on a Shoestring Budget!™ **Invent Inventing** on a Shoestring Budget!™ **Inventing** on a Shoestring Budget!™ **Inventing** on a string Budget! **Inventing** on a Shoestring Budget!™ **Inventing** on a Shoestring Budget!™ **Invent Inventing** on a Shoestring Budget!™ **Inventing** on a Shoestring Budget!™ **Inventing** on a string Budget! **Inventing** on a Shoestring Budget!™ **Inventing** on a Shoestring Budget!™ **Invent Inventing** on a Shoestring Budget!™ **Inventing** on a Shoestring Budget!™ **Inventing** on a

Inventing on a Shoestring Budget!
DISCOUNT COUPON
Patent Search International

$25 OFF the already low price of only $250 for a thorough professional patent search with a legal opinion of patentability! If you have selected a name for your product they will even include a trademark search for no additional charge! With this coupon the cost to you is only $225!

www.patentsearchinternational.com

Patent Search International
PO Box 176 Crownsville, MD 21032
1-410-987-4511   1-800-616-IDEA

Original coupon only! -No photocopies or reproductions - One coupon per submission

---

Inventing on a Shoestring Budget!
DISCOUNT COUPON
Patent Search International

$25 OFF the already low price of only $250 for a thorough professional patent search with a legal opinion of patentability! If you have selected a name for your product they will even include a trademark search for no additional charge! With this coupon the cost to you is only $225!

www.patentsearchinternational.com

Patent Search International
PO Box 176 Crownsville, MD 21032
1-410-987-4511   1-800-616-IDEA

Original coupon only! -No photocopies or reproductions - One coupon per submission

---

Inventing on a Shoestring Budget!
DISCOUNT COUPON
Patent Search International

$25 OFF the already low price of only $250 for a thorough professional patent search with a legal opinion of patentability! If you have selected a name for your product they will even include a trademark search for no additional charge! With this coupon the cost to you is only $225!

www.patentsearchinternational.com

Patent Search International
PO Box 176 Crownsville, MD 21032
1-410-987-4511   1-800-616-IDEA

Original coupon only! -No photocopies or reproductions - One coupon per submission

Inventing on a Shoestring Budget! **Inventing** on a Shoestring Budget! **Inventing** on a string Budget! **Inventing** on a Shoestring Budget! **Inventing** on a Shoestring Budget! **Invent** **Inventing** on a Shoestring Budget! **Inventing** on a Shoestring Budget! **Inventing** on a string Budget! **Inventing** on a Shoestring Budget! **Inventing** on a Shoestring Budget! **Invent** **Inventing** on a Shoestring Budget! **Inventing** on a Shoestring Budget! **Inventing** on a string Budget! **Inventing** on a Shoestring Budget! **Inventing** on a Shoestring Budget! **Invent** **Inventing** on a Shoestring Budget! **Inventing** on a Shoestring Budget! **Inventing** on a string Budget! **Inventing** on a Shoestring Budget! **Inventing** on a Shoestring Budget! **Invent** **Inventing** on a Shoestring Budget! **Inventing** on a Shoestring Budget! **Inventing** on a string Budget! **Inventing** on a Shoestring Budget! **Inventing** on a Shoestring Budget! **Invent** **Inventing** on a Shoestring Budget! **Inventing** on a Shoestring Budget! **Inventing** on a string Budget! **Inventing** on a Shoestring Budget! **Inventing** on a Shoestring Budget! **Invent** **Inventing** on a Shoestring Budget! **Inventing** on a Shoestring Budget! **Inventing** on a string Budget! **Inventing** on a Shoestring Budget! **Inventing** on a Shoestring Budget! **Invent** **Inventing** on a Shoestring Budget! **Inventing** on a Shoestring Budget! **Inventing** on a string Budget! **Inventing** on a Shoestring Budget! **Inventing** on a Shoestring Budget! **Invent** **Inventing** on a Shoestring Budget! **Inventing** on a Shoestring Budget! **Inventing** on a string Budget! **Inventing** on a Shoestring Budget! **Inventing** on a Shoestring Budget! **Invent** **Inventing** on a Shoestring Budget! **Inventing** on a Shoestring Budget! **Inventing** on a string Budget! **Inventing** on a Shoestring Budget! **Inventing** on a Shoestring Budget! **Invent** **Inventing** on a Shoestring Budget! **Inventing** on a Shoestring Budget! **Inventing** on a string Budget! **Inventing** on a Shoestring Budget! **Inventing** on a Shoestring Budget! **Invent** **Inventing** on a Shoestring Budget! **Inventing** on a Shoestring Budget! **Inventing** on a string Budget! **Inventing** on a Shoestring Budget! **Inventing** on a Shoestring Budget! **Invent** **Inventing** on a Shoestring Budget! **Inventing** on a Shoestring Budget! **Inventing** on a string Budget! **Inventing** on a Shoestring Budget! **Inventing** on a Shoestring Budget! **Invent** **Inventing** on a Shoestring Budget! **Inventing** on a Shoestring Budget! **Inventing** on a

To order additional copies of **INVENTING** **On A Shoestring Budget**™!

Mail Check Orders Only:

Second Sight Publishing
PO Box 251248
Plano, TX 75025-0248

Please send the following books:

Quantity:	Title	Price	Total
_____	*Inventing on a Shoestring Budget*™	$15.00	_____

Tax _____
(Texas Residents Only)
Shipping & Handling _____
($3.50 for first book, $1.50 ea. add'l)
TOTAL _____

Ship to:

Name_____

Street_____

City_____State_____Zip_____

We offer quantity discounts for orders of more than 20 books.
For information contact us at barb@asktheinventors.com